Bark Staving Ronkers

To order additional copies, please contact us.
BookSurge, LLC
www.booksurge.com
1-866-308-6235
orders@booksurge.com

JOHN BOBIN

BARK STAVING RONKERS

A Music Memoir

2006

Bark Staving Ronkers

To Alan
& Jerry (My Fruity
Friend!)

With Best Wishes

from

CONTENTS

Dedication and thanks		ix
1.	Scene setting	1
2.	A difficult choice	3
3.	The Phantoms	9
4.	Rhythm and Blues (R&B) and Rock and Roll	21
5.	The Shades	23
6.	The Orioles	27
7.	The Paramounts	31
8.	The Cricketers Inn and other early haunts	37
9.	Jess Conrad and Rhet Stoller	43
10.	Antoinette and The Fingers	47
11.	The Elms	53
12.	The Cliffs Pavilion	61
13.	Peter Eden	63
14.	Polydor	67
15.	Columbia	71
16.	As Psychedelic as Ken Dodd	87
17.	Nigel Grog – "The hardest working man in show business."	89
18.	Three Irish beauties and other adventures	105
19.	Mickie Most loses out!	113
20.	"Beat, Beat, Beat"	115
21.	Legend and the "Red Boot" on Vertigo	137
22.	An old face and more college gigs	163
23.	Moonshine and Matthew Fisher	165
24.	The Italian job	171
25.	Epilogue	179
26.	Reference Sources	183

Dedication and thanks

I have had so much help, advice and friendship over the years that it is difficult to know where to start. My Mum and Dad always encouraged me and put up with me practicing and playing loud music for years at home.
I have had a chequered (but always interesting!) love life and have been married three times, with many ups and downs along the way. I always say that my third wife, Pauline is my last and best wife but a friend has advised me that I should really introduce her as my 'current' wife to keep her on her toes! God bless her anyway, she has helped me by listening patiently (most of the time!) to my ramblings about music and musical friends.

The members of the main bands that I was in between 1960 and 1972, all mentioned in this memoir, ('The Phantoms', 'The Fingers' and 'Legend') all deserve credit for their positive and creative influence and lasting friendship during some exciting but exhausting times.

As I have been researching for this book I have been dismayed and surprised to see how many of the musicians and singers that are featured are no longer with us. I should like to pay tribute to them too.

I should like to dedicate this book to my father, Don Bobin, who died of cancer in 1982 and am donating the profits from this book after paying the tax man (if there are any!) to cancer research.

Cancer Research UK has four main objectives:
- *To carry out world-class research into the biology and causes of cancer.*
- *To develop effective treatments and improve the quality of life for cancer patients.*
- *To reduce the number of people getting cancer.*
- *To provide authoritative information on cancer.*
Research is expensive. Their scientific investment is getting on for £200,000,000 per annum and most of this is raised through voluntary donations. Whether you buy this book or not I urge you to send some money to them. Remember that your donation might be the one that finally provides an answer.

1.
Scene Setting

The music scene in the sixties was incredible. Everywhere you went there was live music. In every bar, club, pub and function room young musicians were given the chance to perfect their music and to pay their dues before recording and touring further afield.

This is in sharp contrast to some of the 'manufactured' bands of today, who sometimes gain experience and broaden their talents *after* becoming well known just for looking good or maybe because they move well.

The live music and the records of the time had exuberance, spontaneity and a spark that is sadly missing in the music of today. A musician friend of mine maintains that Disco music was 'the beginning of the end' and there are many people that would agree.

This book seeks to describe a relatively short period of 12 years or so when I was involved in some early bands of mine that never made it but which did have something to offer.

The musicians that were in these bands are still around and most of them still play, but it was in those early days that they formed opinions about music and how it should be played that have stood them in good stead over the last 40 plus years.

***

Please read and enjoy this humble offering. I have never written a book before and I hope that I can do justice to a musical period that is fondly remembered by many fans of sixties sounds. If I have not captured that spirit what the hell; I'm only a bass player! I have relied heavily on my memory and some (thankfully extensive) scrapbooks to describe the bands with whom I played during this period.

I have also used the Internet in order to try to find out more about various other bands and personalities with whom we came into contact. The reference sources are shown in a separate section of this book for those of you who may wish to learn more.

I do hope that any information, which I offer herein, is as accurate as possible but if there are any errors, please may I apologise in advance. My aim was to show a picture of an era and its atmosphere and I hope you will find this book to be interesting.

2.
A Difficult Choice

When you are only a scruffy 12 year old with only a modicum of the readies the choice between two hot favourites as your first purchase of a 45 r.p.m. single record weighs heavily on your mind. Should it be the mean and magnificent *Apache* by 'The Shadows' or a catchy instrumental version of *Perfidia* by 'The Ventures'?

Standing in the record shop I decided to listen to both of them in the listening booths that they used to have, with semi sound-proof hoods and individual record players for each booth. I suppose I knew deep down what the choice would be even before I checked by hearing each disc over and over again. There was really no contest in the end as 'The Shads' (as they were known to us knowledgeable aficionados) were home grown and I already had a hamfisted knowledge of the opening chords of their monster hit *Apache*.

My pal at school, Steve Porter, had a small 'Burns Trisonic' guitar and could actually play the thing! It was he who had showed me the intro to *Apache* and from that moment on I just knew that I wanted to be a guitarist.

This made me a part of a not very elite band of thousands of other kids who all envied the young lads that were in some cases not very much older than they were, but who were already stars, like 'The Shadows.' Their lead guitarist, Hank Marvin was a major influence on British guitar heroes of the

60's (and later!). Even 'The Beatles' recorded a testament to 'The Shadows' with the only John Lennon/George Harrison collaboration *Cry For A Shadow*.

Much later, in 1996, a CD album was released called Twang on which guitarists like Ritchie Blackmore, Peter Frampton, Peter Green, Tony Iommi, Mark Knopfler, Brian May, Andy Summers and Neil Young all offered their versions of tunes originally recorded by 'The Shadows.'

'The Shadows' were the most famous of all the instrumental groups in England at that time and Hank was a joy to behold with his red 'Fender Stratocaster' (which had been ordered by mistake when he wanted a guitar like the one used by James Burton on Rick Nelson's records) and his trademark horn rimmed specs.

Even to this day there are many 'Shadows' tribute bands such as 'The Rapiers' (great band!) and there are groups of 'Shadows' fans that meet regularly so they can play with each other or to backing tracks. The obligatory 'Fenders' are always in evidence but by now these players all know that they want to play a 'Stratocaster' rather than the 'Telecaster' as favoured by James Burton. Another guitarist that was influenced by Hank was Eric Clapton. Eric described Hank as: 'Unbeatable!'

'The Shadows' also backed Cliff Richard, before he was a virgin, but my real interest was in 'The Shads', not the rather bland Mr. Richard. Hank had wisely adopted his stage name rather than use his real but non-Rock and Roll moniker Brian.

'The Shadows' had also perfected a stage act that included the intricate and difficult to master 'Shadow walk', a backwards and forwards circular confection that many another group tried to perfect and few did! It was only much later that I read somewhere that this had been copied from another American act –'The Treniers'. Another aspect was a high kicking routine in numbers like *FBI,* which had yet to be released.

I bought *Apache* and from then on music would form a huge part of my life. When I was a young teenager every waking minute seemed to be crammed with groups, music and guitars. Learning to play numbers by ear in those days was a repetitive process which even included playing 45's at 33 r.p.m. in order to make it easier to learn fast passages. Conversely playing singles at 78 r.p.m. so the bass lines could be heard in their new temporary higher register was another way of getting to grips with the bass parts.

This was way before the current trend of mixing the bass high in the end product and it was not always easy to spot the way that a bass player had played on the records of the time. Bass players like Jet Harris (of 'The Shadows') were also very inventive and often played different phrases in the repeated sections of the tune. It was a matter of personal pride to play exactly what was on the record, or more likely what we thought was on the record. Jet was the first person in Britain to use an electric bass guitar and it is heartening to see that he is still playing today. At one 'Shadowmania' event (organised by Bruce Welch, the ex-rhythm guitarist of 'The Shadows') Jet joked that he did not think he could keep it up for much longer! His opening remark to an ecstatic audience was: 'Have you all got your heating allowance?'

For the benefit of young readers, or even those who have forgotten what a massive influence Hank Marvin had on the early 'beat' groups I think it is safe to say that he was a role model for all our great guitar heroes. Hank Marvin (lead guitar), Bruce Welch, (rhythm guitar), Jet Harris (bass guitar) and Tony Meehan (drums) formed the classic 'Shadows' line up at the time. Many other great musicians have played with

'The Shadows' through the years and they played a 'final' UK tour in 2004 with three of the stalwarts, Hank, Bruce and Brian Bennett; a "new boy" who only replaced Tony Meehan in 1962!

Brian's son, Warren Bennett is also a fine musician, playing guitar, bass and keyboards and he has been a regular with Hank Marvin's touring band until fairly recently, when Hank announced that he was retiring. (Hank has also had the benefit of his own son's guitar playing in his touring band and Ben Marvin is an example of how music must be in the genes.) Warren Bennett also plays in 'The Vibratos' with Dick Plant. Dick is another good guitarist and he used to engineer for 'The Shadows' when they were recording together wayback when. Hank Marvin was and is possibly the only guitarist that has an instantly recognisable style and sound, although anybody who has seen one of his live shows will know that he is capable of playing very convincingly in many styles.

But where was I? I took my record of *Apache* home and proceeded to bore the whole family silly by playing the same tune over and over again while trying to memorise how it went. I then started nagging my long-suffering parents for a guitar and an amp. Eventually my Mum and Dad weakened and bought me a peculiar German 'Hopf' guitar in a hammered pink finish complemented by a small (and very quiet) 'Baird' amp. A TV manufacturer made the 'Baird' amplifiers and this particular amp pushed out a huge 5 watts! 'Hopf' guitars were made in Germany from the late 1950's onwards and were produced until the 80's. They made solid, semi-solid and archtop guitars.

'Hofner' was another of the European guitar makers that made good quality guitars for those of us that could not afford a 'Fender.' Other makes hanging on the walls of the music shops included 'Framus', 'Hoyer', 'Klira' and others plus the usual custom made jobs. Apparently these companies often shared parts from the same suppliers. This would explain why you could see the same tailpieces, bridges, tuners, and inlays on rival guitar makes.

3.
The Phantoms

My first guitar and amp were purchased from a second hand shop in a back street in Southend run by Keith Butchart (Butch) from whence he would sell anything to anybody at any time. Butch was a huge hairy man and played guitar half sitting, half lying on an old car seat in his tatty emporium. Butch was multi-talented, being a pianist, guitarist and dabbler in other instruments and was eventually the person who got my very first band The Phantoms their first gig at the RAFA Hall in Southend.

The Phantoms at the RAFA Hall Southend - 1962 (L to R)
Mark Mills, Steve Porter, Bob Clouter, John Bobin

Butch also played in a piano, double bass and drums trio called 'Les Pecheurs.' One day the band was waiting to be paid and the man with the money was heard to say: 'OK which one of you is Les?' Butch was also the person who taught my oldest pal Mark Mills and me our first tunes on the guitar and they were: *Never On A Sunday* and *Lady Be Good.* Mark's Dad had already shown us some rudimentary chords on ukuleles for songs such as *Hang Down Your Head Tom Dooley* but we really wanted to move up a gear and to become pukka guitarists.

My purchase of *Apache* (on the well known green 'Columbia' label) was made at a local music store that sold records and sheet music downstairs and musical instruments upstairs. 'The Shadows' were the very first British group to be awarded a Gold Disc (for *Apache.*) They were presented with it on the 'Thank Your Lucky Stars' TV programme in April 1962.

My buddies and I gradually started to virtually live in the music shop mentioned above, 'Gilbert's Pianos', and both the manager and his staff were amazingly patient with this crowd of grubby kids who would eventually spend money there, but not for some time! One of the sales assistants was a trumpeter by the name of Bert Collier, who would in time help one of the UK's leading jazz trumpeters, Digby Fairweather to develop his unique style.

I wanted to play like Hank, but so did everybody else. No, I really wanted to be Hank. There was however, a small problem in the way. He was a good guitarist and I wasn't. I played lead guitar for a few months and together with Mark Mills (whom I had known since we were five years old and who now lives in sunny Espana) we did a few parties where we would play all the tunes we knew and then play them all again.

I had another pal at school called Ken Leftwich (Lefty) who had already proved that he had talent by mastering *Apache* and eventually other tunes by our favourite band, 'The Shadows.' He also had a guitar and wanted to join this duo that I had formed with Mark. (We used to call Mark 'Millsy.' He always used to say:

'Don't call me Millsy' and so of course we did.) Mark was quite content at that time to play rhythm although he later played lead, and very ably too, in many bands. At this time though Mark modelled his style on Bruce Welch and would later tackle the cripplingly fast part for *The Savage.* He would attempt this guitar part whilst standing sideways on with his cherry red 'Hofner' guitar, which for some reason he called George, pointing upwards like 'The Shads' did in live performances of *Apache.* Mark Mills had cultivated a floppy quiff that gradually subsided whilst he was playing, so by the end of a number he probably couldn't see what he was doing anyway.

Fate intervened and I agreed to become a bass guitarist so we could recruit young Lefty with his home made electronic guitars, amps and more importantly...specs. Many guitarists in the early sixties wore Hank style horn rimmed spectacles and they all thought that they looked the bees' knees. Some of them wore them even though they did not need them The irony of it is that Hank now wears specs on stage but elsewhere he wears contact lenses.

With Lefty on lead, Mark on rhythm and me on bass we knew, just knew, that we were going to be the new 'Shadows.' Lefty had an intense personality and his drive for perfection meant that before every number he would be playing a few notes with one tone setting and then with another, repeating the whole process with different echo flavours until he was convinced that the sound was exactly like Hank's sound on a particular track. Nowadays musicians still copy sounds and echo effects/repeats but they have digital modelling to make life easier.

We had a mixture of amps and at one time I used a 'Trebletone Major' amp with no housing at all and a 'Wharfedale' speaker cabinet that seemed huge but probably only housed a 12" speaker. Later we used a 'Vox AC10' for the whole band: lead, bass, rhythm and even for vocals so that must have been a pretty awful sound! Mark's dad made him a huge amp, which he rolled down the drive of his parents' bungalow after gigs, on inbuilt castors, which were quite a rarity in those days. Rumbling this monster down the concrete drive in the small hours probably made Mark very popular with his poor neighbours.

Another friend at school was Bob Clouter. (What a name for a drummer and it is his real name too.) Bob was a young and personable chap with a tendency to puppy fat but he had a wicked dry sense of humour. Bob had also developed the obligatory quiff and managed to produce the required dip in the middle of the front of his hair. My hair was still recalcitrant and just would not go back. I was very jealous of the guys who could get that Tony Curtis/James Dean quiff. Bob Clouter told me that he was a real drummer and that he had a drum kit. Both of these statements were 'ever so slightly' stretching the truth. He had played a bass drum in a local boys' organisation but that was the real extent of his drumming experience. However, he was our mate and we needed a drummer so he was in. He then persuaded his long suffering Dad (Big Bob) to buy him a snare drum, a stand and a cymbal and hey – we were now really cooking.

Most groups of the day wore smart suits but our budget

was very limited as we were all schoolboys, so we bought some grey and white striped shirts, which we complemented with natty downturned V bow ties with a pearl button in the middle. Rehearsals were held at our parents' homes and at the time my Dad was having a new garage built at the end of our garden so we used to practice in the half built shell of this building sometimes.

Like many young sixties bands we started playing at Youth Clubs and would take our gear to rehearsals and unpaid gigs by bus. Gradually our repertoire widened so that we played non-'Shadows' material too. These new tunes included numbers by 'The Moon-Trekkers', 'The Hunters', 'The Cougars' and 'Nero and The Gladiators'. We even tried some squeaky vocals.

Adam Faith had a good band, 'The Roulettes', with Russ Ballard on guitar and we played a few of their songs as well as the odd Cliff Richard number. But it was 'The Beatles' that really changed our repertoire and we must have made an extraordinary sound trying to emulate the more gritty parts of their style.

Some of our first performances were at Talent Shows. I remember that one was at 'The Kursaal Ballroom' on Southend seafront. We didn't win but we did enjoy the friendly camaraderie between the contestants, who included a band in which the guitarist was Bob Heath (with whom I later teamed up when we backed Jess Conrad.)

The Klimax at The Kursaal Southend – 1964 (L to R)
Mark Mills, John Bobin, Bob Clouter, Ken 'Lefty' Leftwich

Another Talent Show offering was at 'The Cliffs Bandstage' in Westcliff (near Southend) and we were astonished when the audience ran away as soon as we started to play. This was explained to us later. The people concerned had been sitting in the open air and it had started to rain!

More gigs followed, including a weekly residency at a drinking club on Southend sea front, 'The Coq D'Or.' The patrons were very kind to us and adopted us as their favourite group even though we were still spotty young teenagers. I think that the club probably offered other types of entertainment to patrons who wanted to go upstairs for some horizontal jogging. We wrote our first tune, *The Coq D'Or Stomp* at this time but I cannot recall how it went.

We experimented with different names like 'The

Thunderbeats', 'The Klimax' and many other weird and (thankfully) mostly temporary aberrations. A girl in the audience asked us one night how we managed to keep a climax going all night. If we could do that now we would make our fortune.

At 'Southend High School for Boys', which was the school that was the seat of learning for Lefty, Bob and myself, we also had a younger friend who at that time was still known as Martin Birch, but whom later on metamorphosed into Will Birch of 'The Kursaal Flyers.' Will showed later that he could pen songs that had a sharp sense of humour about them. 'The Kursaal Flyers' (named after a fake train that was used during the carnivals at Southend) enjoyed some success, later on even having a number 15 hit in 1976 with a Will Birch song *Little Does She Know.* 'The Kursaal Flyers' (or 'The Kursaals' for short) were also formed in Southend, and Jonathan King signed them to his label, 'UK.' *Chocs Away* and *The Great Artiste"* were very good albums and they featured snappy pop songs. Their high point was achieved after joining 'CBS' Records when *Little Does She Know* was a chart success. They issued another album in 1976 called, *Golden Mile* that was produced by Mike Batt. In 1977 Graeme Douglas (their very able lead guitarist) left and he then joined 'Eddie and the Hotrods.' Douglas' replacement was Barry Martin. Barry was originally a good drummer but one day he ditched his sticks and vowed to become a guitarist instead. (Barry now heads up 'The Hamsters', a loud and excellent Hendrix style power trio.) 'The Kursaals' split up following a live album, *Five Live Kursaals.* Will Birch played with other bands like 'The Records', but after compiling the album *In For A Spin,* 'The Kursaals' were back together again for *Former Tour De Force Is Forced To Tour.* They have been touring again recently and are still received well by today's audiences.

'The Kursaals' also had a fine pedal steel guitarist who was later a member of 'Hunt Runt Shunt and Cunningham' (see later, much later) but who was, like us learning to play guitar in the magic sixties.

My first bass was a one cut away, dung brown 'Dallas Tuxedo.' This was a small bass and I believe it was also the first model used by ace sessioneer Mo Foster. I always thought that this guitar was German made, but I now understand that the 'Dallas Tuxedo' was the first British made solid guitar, narrowly beating the 'Watkins Rapier' to that honour by a couple of weeks. The guitars that everybody wanted though, were the pure bred American dazzlers like 'Fenders', 'Gibsons' and 'Gretsch' instruments. I named my 'Dallas Tuxedo', Denise, after very nice blonde lass who was my girlfriend at the time. I didn't realise then that other more famous and much more proficient musicians also called their instruments after their current squeezes. (The best example is B B King and his guitar Lucille.) The 'Tuxedo' was truly awful but it was my very first bass and I played it with as much panache as I could muster, with a plastic skeleton attached to the headstock. Please don't ask me why, because I can't think of any good reason. No, I can't even think of a bad one.

I next purchased a 'Rosetti Lucky 7' bass guitar like one of Paul McCartney's early basses, although I don't know if his was the same virulent shade of green that mine was. The 'Rosetti' was involved in an accident at a wedding that we were playing at when the bride tripped over my lead and the plastic scratch plate with an integral lead, was snapped in two.

Eventually I progressed to a 'Hofner Verithin' bass, (a German bass) which was bright red, had two cut-aways and was an altogether sexier looking beast than the 'Tuxedo.' 'Hofners' were well made and are now collectors' items. I recently met a chap who has over thirty of these guitars in various different models. He started collecting them some time ago when they were going for a song and is now amazed at the value of his set of 'Hofners.' The 'Verithin' was my first nice guitar and was also a more modern looking instrument than my previous basses. I bought my 'Verithin' from a music shop in London somewhere that was recommended to me by a very quiet and young lad named Dave Mattacks who was a new boy at our school. Dave was an unassuming fair-haired boy with glasses who wore a suede jacket and for a time had the nickname 'Suede L'Inconnu.' Wonder of wonders, Dave was also a drummer and his band 'The Five Star Combo' (later known as 'Phase Five') played at 'The Coq D'Or' too. Dave went on to be a long-term member of 'Fairport Convention' and became a very well respected session drummer. Dave Mattacks has ably filled the drum seat for well known names such as Joan Armatrading, Gary Brooker, Elkie Brooks, Mary Chapin-Carpenter, Beverley Craven, Sandy Denny, Barbara Dickson, Brian Eno, 'Everything but the Girl', Georgie Fame and many more.

The guys in 'The Phantoms' (who had probably become 'The Klimax' by now) had become friendly with some girls from Southend High School for Girls and in some cases we had the same girls (not usually at the same time) as our girlfriends, in quick and baffling succession. One of these girls was Pam Ffitch who was dark, sultry and incredibly sexy. Pam went out with Mark first but I am pleased to say that she became my girlfriend later. We would spend many happy hours in a room in her parents' house which was wood panelled and had been used previously as a ballet room. The records we played stay in my mind to this day. Because we had so few, we used to play then over and over again. *Lipstick On Your Collar* by Connie Francis, *Go Away Little Girl* by Mark Wynter and *Til I Kissed*

Her by 'The Everly Brothers' were some of these 'discs' as they called them then.

Another girl became Mark's special girl friend and this lass, Pam Wallace, had also helped us back in our duo days by supplying bass lines on her piano when we were rehearsing. Later, she and I spent some time together at the end of each school holiday when Mark had to go back to school a day earlier than us and we used to cuddle and flirt but we didn't entirely let Mark down!

One of the strangest places that 'The Phantoms' played at was at a Yacht Club in what used to be 'Old Leigh Railway Station.' I remember that we were playing more and more Rock and Roll and that night we were playing snatches of songs like *Tutti Fruitti* and other Little Richard ditties, as we didn't know all the words.

The coffee bars that were frequented by youngsters had previously experimented with various kinds of music and for example, the beatniks had adopted Trad Jazz as their own. These Beatniks had beards and duffle coats (the lads) and long hair and duffle coats (the birds) and were heavily into the 'Campaign for Nuclear Disarmament' or 'CND'. 'CND' campaigns non-violently to rid the world of nuclear weapons and believes that they can change Government policies and bring about a much more public debate about nuclear weapons. Its members and supporters fund the organisation. Trad Jazz to me always sounds like everybody playing exactly what they want to over everybody else's lines i.e. a complete mess. A friend of mine always says that jazz starts off as very nice tunes, has some meaningless noodling in the middle and then goes back to proper melody lines.

The records that Pam Ffitch and I played were far simpler

but they were still the anodyne face of pop and I was soon to have a real revelation when I discovered American Rhythm and Blues (R&B) and Rock and Roll.

4.
Rhythm and Blues (R&B) and Rock and Roll

At about this time (1963 or so) my first experiences of Rhythm and Blues (R&B) and Rock and Roll changed my musical orientation. Two local bands, and it's fair to say, two local singers in particular, made me realise that this was the sound that I now wanted to be producing.

The coffee bars of Southend were polarised into what eventually became Mods' and Rockers' haunts. I drifted around several like the Jacobean and the Capri. I really wanted to be a Mod but was too young so I hung around with real Mods who were older and cooler as well as my contemporaries. The Mod movement seemed to have been gathering momentum for a little while before the press latched on to the new phenomenon, in about 1962. Parkas, Lambretta and Vespa scooters and pop art all played their own parts in the overall development of the Mods. They were also snappy dressers under the Parkas! The first Levis that I ever wore were made from uncomfortable and stiff, heavy denim, but they were a badge, which showed that you belonged. Desert boots were also popular (although they were later eschewed for 'Hush Puppies.') The drug scene was comparatively tame compared to today's problems but those who wanted to try something different traded 'purple hearts' in the coffee bars. These were 'pep' pills and were a staple recreational drug in the early-mid 60s, and the drug of choice for the Mod crowd. They were widely used by those who did not want to move on to worse options (which were around but which were not to my knowledge as widely used by the teenagers as they are today.) Mod bands such as 'The Small Faces' and 'The Who' were extremely popular with these youngsters.

If you were not a Mod, you could be a Rocker. These guys were either dressed as latter-day James Dean clones or they were bedecked in Teddy Boy finery. Gene Vincent, Eddie Cochran and early Elvis were the most popular singers for the Rockers. Rockers still congregate at Rock and Roll weekenders sometimes, at Holiday Camps. Rockers' favourite music was Rock and Roll or Rockabilly and they were generally reckoned to be tough guys and they thought that Mods were namby pambies. Fights between the rival factions were very common and sometimes they drew up battle lines at seaside resorts on bank holidays.

Youngsters at this time had a very limited choice of appetisers in these haunts and expresso coffee; hot chocolate and soggy beef burgers more or less exhausted the imagination of the owners' menus for the coffee bars. The main attractions however were the jukeboxes and the company.

5.
The Shades

The real jewel in the crown of the local coffee bars in the Southend area was without a doubt 'The Shades', on Southend sea front. I was asked some time ago to provide a recollection of 'The Shades' for Procol Harum's web site 'Beyond the Pale.' This site is a real labour of love for many Procol Harum fans and is a huge source of information about PH and their changing personnel over the years. I recommend it wholeheartedly! Here is what I wrote in its entirety:

"A Southend Shade of Pale"
In the dim and distant early Sixties a favourite haunt of mine was 'The Shades.' Set on Southend sea front this coffee bar, owned and run by Robin Trower's parents, was a magnet for 'Mods' and wannabes who frequented a 'club' no more than a few doors away from a 'Rocker' equivalent. Surprisingly 'The Shades' also attracted a fanatical Rock'n'Roll contingent who widened their musical horizons to include esoteric American Pop, R'n'B and Blues by some well-known and lesser names from the States.

The jukebox at 'The Shades' had the odd 'token' English disc (such as the earthy *She's in Love with a Teenage Idol* by the 'Laurie Jay Combo') but the main musical direction was across the pond. At Christmas the featured record was *Run Run Rudolph* by Chuck Berry (who else?) and the atmosphere at 'The Shades' was even more electric.

On Sundays 'The Paramounts' held court on a tiny stage downstairs, where all the walls had been lovingly (but not very effectively) soundproofed with egg boxes. At the back of the stage was a cartoon mural of 'The Paramounts' on which some wag had scribed comments.

'The Paramounts' went through many changes in their on stage apparel but one that I recall was a set of smart suede waistcoats. Another was the wearing of striped blazers.

As a young and inexperienced bass guitarist myself I happily paid my one shilling and sixpence (7 1/2 pence) and stood transfixed during 'The Paramounts' sets. Gradually I came to know and love this heady mix of Rock'n'Roll, Blues and eccentric selections of American Pop music. (The repertoire was wonderful!)

The upright piano took a severe punishing, particularly during Jerry Lee Lewis numbers - Gary doing battle with the poor submissive instrument whilst his musical cohorts thundered away behind him. Diz Derrick was one of the few bass players I had seen using an 'Epiphone Rivoli.' This was a departure from the norm as the 'Fender Precision' was pretty much the industry standard. The 'Rivolis' deep and full tones supplemented Barrie Wilson's *enormous* drum style perfectly. (This was pre the 'BJ' tag.) Barrie seemed to smile continuously - he was enjoying himself so much. As the baby of the band it is particularly saddening to remember his untimely departure from the World's 'stage'. Rob (or Robbie) Trower played a 'Gretsch Country Gent' guitar in a way that its manufacturer had surely never envisaged. (The more formal 'Robin' stage persona emerged later.) Using a Selmer 'Little Giant' as crude but gutsy sounding pre-amp, the over-driven bluesy sound was a radical change from the ubiquitous Hank Marvin sound that was everywhere else. Separately then, the individual members of the band were great. But together, the whole band kicked arse and perfectly complemented Gary's wonderfully expressive voice. Their early recordings give some idea of the raw sound and power of the group, but their live performance was the tops. Along the way changes were made, such as a better PA, the usage of a Hohner Pianet instead of the unreliable house pianos, the temporary change to a different drummer, but the band really cooked. Their repertoire widened and they experimented with new material; for example early James Brown numbers featured heavily at one time. I have followed Gary and his peers' careers with interest and remember well a girlfriend of mine enthusing over *A Whiter Shade of Pale* (which at that time I had not heard.) 'What's it like?' I asked. 'It's not like anything else,' she puzzled. A tatty Chinese restaurant ('The Flying Dragon') above a market arcade in Southend had this diverting tribute to 'The Paramounts' scribbled on the wall of the toilet: A mistaken scrawler had written 'The Paramounts are shit.' Underneath the rejoinder from a Paramounts' devotee was: 'Superlative of course!'

You can find out more about the early 'Procol Harum' on the fine site that is lovingly tended by these 'PH' addicts (or Procholics) by going to:

www.procolharum.com

But back to the guys that effectively (and temporarily) weaned me off 'The Shadows'. I say temporarily because although as a teenager I either loved or hated a sound to the exclusion of all others, as an old git I now have an extended appreciation of many different types of music.

6.
The Orioles

There were two local groups that used to play at 'The Shades' weekly. In the week there was 'The Orioles', but on a Sunday the whole place was always packed for 'The Paramounts.' 'The Orioles' were named thus by Gary Brooker (leader of 'The Paramounts' and later the main man for 'Procol Harum.') He took the name 'The Orioles' from a Bobby Day song from 1958, which became a staple part of their repertoire, *Rocking Robin.* This same song was made into a semi-novelty hit by Michael Jackson years later in 1972. The line up of 'The Orioles' was not the usual three guitars and drums that I had accepted as the norm. Bashing away at a piano Jerry Lee Lewis style was the forte of 'The Orioles' singer Mick (later Mickey) Jupp. Mick was also at my old school but is a few years older than I am. He had fiery red hair and flailed away at the keyboard like a demented younger brother of Jerry Lee and even included the odd few notes played elbow style or with the toe of a boot. He was yet to feature his distinctive guitar style on stage but had already become a great singer with a forceful view of what was good and what was bad in terms of music and its presentation. He was also one of the first people that I had ever met that was a 'Star Trek' fan. I remember that Mick was the first one of my friends to call me John rather than Johnny, although he went the other way by becoming Mickey when he was called Mick by most if not all of his friends when I fist knew him. 'The Orioles' also had a very good guitarist who could play like Chet Atkins as well as Chuck Berry. Dougie Sheldrake (for it was he) took to wearing moccasins on stage and would close his eyes as he played the sparkling riffs to R&B songs like *Suzie Q* and *My Babe*. More to the point he played a 'Gretsch Tennessean', not the usual 'Fender Stratocaster' that was played by nearly every wannabe Hank at the time. Bearded, jovial and usually drunk, the bass player was Adrian (Ada) Baggerley who played a ropey 'Guyatone' bass through a 'Fenton Weill' amp. (On the first few 'Shadows' recordings Hank Marvin had also used a 'Guyatone' instrument but his trademark sound really came from the 'Fender Stratocaster.') Boomy low bass was the order of the day for these bands as this filled up the sound nicely and Ada enjoyed himself so much that one night at a local pub he fell over backwards, right over the top of his amp and continued to play lying on his back. (Ada is now no longer with us – RIP.) Bespectacled Tony Diamond was the drummer and was the only person I know who carried an entire drum kit around in a tiny bubble car. When he pulled up at a filling station he had to extricate himself from between the drum cases before he could get out to fill his car up. But Mick Jupp stole the show as he bent over the keyboard of a battered old upright piano at 'The Shades', pretending to be a red headed Jerry Lee. 'The Orioles' had a varied repertoire that included Ernie K Doe and Benny Spellman numbers as well as a few Country flavoured nuggets such as *Sweet Dreams*. They also played R&B and Blues numbers with great gusto. These included gems like *Got Love If You Want It, Got My Mojo Working* and *How Long*. One of their most popular songs was that old Bobby Day number *Rockin' Robin* as mentioned above, and the audience would complete the end line of the middle eight '….the hoppin' boppin buzzard and the: Oriole!' The aim

was to deafen the person next to you by shouting the word
Oriole! as loud as you possibly could and this song is still used
by Mickey as his closing song on live gigs.

7.
The Paramounts

On Sundays 'The Shades' rocked to 'The Paramounts.' Gary Brooker played Rock and Roll and R&B on the same rough old piano that Mick punished during the week. Both Mick and Gary had a presence and a vocal quality that was unusual in those days in spite of their youth. Gary was a very young man to be able to sing like Ray Charles and had a dark fringe that fell forward as he played the 'joanna,' with a cherubic expression. Gary also suffered from a little adolescent weight at that time and on the cartoon pictures of 'The Paramounts' on the back wall of the stage someone had unkindly scrawled over his torso the words 'Fatty Paramount!' The guitarist with 'The Paramounts' - Robin Trower (usually called Rob or even Robbie in those days) played blues like nobody I had ever seen before on another 'Gretsch', this time an orange 'Country Gentleman.' Robin had blonde hair and another huge fringe, which was the fashion in those days after the young guns stopped combing their hair forward. This followed years of everybody trying to get their hair to stay back and to form a nice quiff over the forehead. Rob's hair was very blonde and perhaps it owed its colour to a bottle. Diz Derrick was the bass player with an 'Epiphone Rivoli' and 'Selmer' amplification, including a huge 'Selmer Goliath' with an 18" bass speaker. His loping, jazzy walking bass style was just great and the 'Rivoli' together with the 'Goliath' made for a low end that was sure to rattle the walls downstairs in 'The Shades.' Finally, there was the baby of the band. This was the good looking and always smiling Barrie (B J) Wilson. Later described as having a style like an "octopus in a bath", Barrie was immensely talented and a key member of 'Procol Harum' for many years. Barrie was a very good-natured chap and will always be missed by those of us that were lucky enough to have known him. (Sadly Barrie is also no longer with us.)

Somewhere along the way, 'The Phantoms' had another guitarist, Steve Porter, the guy with the 'Burns Trisonic' mentioned earlier, a tiny guitar that had pick ups that were later to feature heavily in the sound that Brian May has made his own. This was the same Steve Porter who set me on the road to ruin by teaching me the chords to *Apache*. Steve had callipers on his leg following a very unfortunate playground accident that caused a serious infection in a nasty wound. Steve stayed for a while and then Lefty returned, with yet another of his home made guitars. This one was black, with long horns and three 'Plato' pick-ups. Lefty still has this guitar in his loft but I am pleased to say that the classical guitars he makes nowadays are easier to play and they sound better. The only problem is that they also cost getting on for £3,000 each; but trust me they are worth every penny. We now sang in 'The Phantoms' as well as playing and our repertoire was full of 'Beatles' songs as well as other offerings from other beat groups of the time like 'The Searchers' and 'The Merseybeats.' These complemented the instrumental numbers, which still formed a fair part of our repertoire. At this time we started to incorporate R&B and Rock and Roll numbers, frequently copying songs played by both 'The Orioles' and 'The Paramounts.'

Another group that played at 'The Shades' ('The Flowerpots') had a good chunky guitarist called John Wilkinson, who later changed his name to Wilko Johnson. Wilko used to be a schoolteacher but soon found his real niche as an axe man. Wilko later became a founder member of the pub-rock band 'Dr. Feelgood.' 'Dr. Feelgood' took their name from a 1961 record by another group from the USA, (called 'Dr Feelgood and the Interns'), when they formed their band in 1971. The UK 'Dr Feelgood' band was a leading pub-rock influence and the first line-up was Lee Brilleaux, (vocals/harmonica), Wilko Johnson, John B. Sparks (bass), John Potter (piano) and 'Bandsman' Howarth (drums). When Potter and Howarth left, John 'The Big Figure' Martin joined. 'Dr. Feelgood' came from Canvey Island. In 1974 they signed up with United Artists Records. Lee Brilleaux (RIP) looked extremely aggressive and vicious on stage but he was a real gent off stage. Wilko had the strangest stage act that I had ever seen at the time. He would move across the stage sideways and backwards and forwards. Whilst he was doing this he had his head facing the audience and he would not miss his footing even though he was moving furiously from one part of the stage to another in a jerky and totally manic fashion. 'Dr. Feelgood's' first album was, *Down By The Jetty,* released in 1975, but it was their third album, a live recording, *Stupidity,* that really broke through. Wilko left not long after this album and John "Gypie" Mayo replaced him. 'Dr. Feelgood' continued to play and work hard but it was not until 1979 that they had their only single hit, *Milk And Alcohol.* In 1981 Mayo left and Johnny Guitar replaced him. In 1982 John B Sparks and John Martin decided to leave. Lee Brilleaux disbanded the band, but reformed the outfit after only a few months with Gordon Russell (guitar), Kevin Morris (drums) and Phil Mitchell (bass). The UK audiences were dwindling but they were still popular in the States. At about this time they started their own label, Grand Records.

Gordon Russell left the band and his replacement was Steve Walwyn. Phil Mitchell left during the recording of an album named *Primo* and the brilliant bassist Dave Bronze (who later became a member of Procol Harum) joined in his stead. Very bad news came in 1993, when Lee Brilleaux was diagnosed as having lymphoma and he had to stop touring. Lee died in 1994 having made a final album with 'The Feelgoods'. Lee wanted the band to continue and so Steve Walwyn, Kevin Morris and Phil Mitchell got back together a year later with a new singer, Pete Gage to record *On The Road Again*. Finally, Robert Kane, a vocalist for one of the later versions of The Animals, replaced Gage on the album named *Chess Masters*. This was the band's first album of the new millennium. Wilko, was a good bluesy player when I first saw him, but he eventually modelled his style on the choppy rhythm cum lead playing of Mick Green.

Mick Green first came to prominence in the early '60s, as a member of Johnny Kidd & the Pirates. Many guitarists have copied his unusual style including Pete Townsend and Wilko. Mick Green favoured a Telecaster (like James Burton) and he used this with a 'Fender' amp. He later joined Billy J Kramer's backing group 'The Dakotas'. Mick Green also played for a short time with Cliff Bennett but he later joined Engelbert Humperdinck's backing band and played for him for seven well-paid years.

James Burton, the guitarist who lovingly embellished early Ricky Nelson records, is also a dedicated Telecaster man. In about 1967 'Fender' issued some 'Telecaster' guitars with a paisley finish. These guitars were intended to be attuned to the flower power atmosphere at the time but they were not popular. However, James did adopt this monstrosity. James' country flavoured picking is fast and furious and has also been an influence on other leading guitarists like Albert Lee and

Jerry Donahue. James' most successful job was as Elvis Presley's guitarist during Elvis' fat Las Vegas phase.

From 'The Phantoms' first gig in 1962 at the 'RAFA Hall' we progressed (slowly) to gigs where we were actually paid. (There is a story that we were supposed to get paid at the 'RAFA Hall' but Butch 'forgot' to pass the money on.) We played a few times at 'The Shades' but did not attract the same devotion from the audiences as 'The Paramounts' or 'The Orioles.'

One summer we did a gig at 'Butlin's Holiday Camp' in Bognor Regis for Bob Clouter's father's firm. This was the first time that we had tried rum and blackcurrant. We thought that this awful concoction was the kind of thing that you could knock back without suffering later. Of course we were wrong and duly felt sick as dogs the next day even though we played that morning as well as the previous night.

8.
The Cricketers Inn And Other Early Haunts

The Cricketers Inn' was (and still is at the time of writing) a local pub in Westcliff where there was a dance hall behind the pub. (This hall is now 'The Riga Music Bar.') 'The Orioles' started to play there several times a week. The crowd was friendly, receptive and tough. I spent many a happy evening there and can also recall some lovely ladies and early but interesting teenage fumblings. I won't mention the names of these ladies but thanks for the happy memories!

Another venue in Southend was a dance hall at the back of the long gone 'London Hotel'. One night 'The Orioles' were playing there and a lady who just happened to have a bottle stashed in her handbag offered me some neat gin. I can remember very little about the evening although I seem to recall vomiting all over the waiting room floor at Southend Central railway station whilst trying to converse with another local musician, drummer Rod (Noddy) Nolan. He obviously didn't hold it against me as we played together many years later in a trio called 'Tim Gentle and his Gentlemen.' The next day I went into a local coffee bar and started to be teased by all and sundry. "What about you and Doris (name changed to protect the innocent) then? Where did you two disappear to for such a long time?" Doris, if you are reading this and if you know whom you are I apologise for forgetting whatever it was that we got up to.

I started to stand in on a few numbers occasionally with 'The Orioles' and so did Bob Clouter. After a couple of changes in personnel the main members of my then current band, 'Red Green and his Blues Combo' reversed into 'The Orioles' to form a new version of the band. This band included the guitarist who is generally recognised by all of my friends as the best ever guitarist to emerge from Southend, Maurice (Mo) Witham. Mo Witham also had a 'Gretsch Tennessean' like Dougie Sheldrake and boy could he play. As well as the Rock and Roll and R&B styles he could also play swing music a la Django Reinhardt. He maintained that he learnt the swing numbers while he was asleep by allowing the record player to repeat the tunes over and over again.

'The New Orioles' had a line up as follows: Mickey Jupp, (vocals and piano), Bob Clouter (drums), Mo Witham (lead guitar), Barry Scanling, (rhythm guitar) and me on bass. Barry was a very relaxed character and he coined the phrase "There's too much Rock and not enough Roll," which you will understand if you listen to the old style records that had some swing about them and then compare them to some of the supposed Rock and Roll records that came out later "with not enough Roll." I think he also meant that we should not take things too seriously. 'The New Orioles' (soon called 'The Orioles' again) continued to play at 'The Cricketers' plus anywhere else that would have us. There was music everywhere in those days and it was all live, as this was before the dreaded Karaoke and backing supplied on minidiscs. The venues were not always that posh and we often played upstairs in smallish function rooms over pubs like 'The Middleton' and 'The Castle.' The repertoire that Mick Jupp had played with his previous version of the band was largely repeated with the new band and was the perfect antidote to the generally bland material that was popular in those days. 'The Orioles' auditioned for an agency headed up by a well known agent, Maurice King, at a club in the West End and were pleased to see 'The Walker Brothers' in the audience apparently enjoying our brand of music that was so different to their power ballads. The outcome of the audition was that Mick was asked to record a cover of *Stagger Lee* for 'Decca' but the other 'Orioles' were told that session musicians would be used for the recording. We were a little upset by this but it was common practice at that time to use well-known, and in all honesty, extremely good sessioneers for records that were allegedly recorded by young and fairly inexperienced muso's.

Brilliant session guitarists (experienced heavy weight musos) such as the legendary Vick Flick (of the James Bond theme fame), Joe Morretti and Big Jim Sullivan played on many sessions for groups that did not appear on their 'own' records. In this way the record companies could ensure that the recording sessions, usually only lasting for three hours, produced the right sounds to a high level of musicality. Guitar heroes such as Jimmy Page and Jeff Beck also played on many a record for other, and often much less talented artists in the mid sixties.

Big Jim Sullivan was probably the most prolific session guitarist ever. He had at least 1,000 chart entries and was one of the most sought after session guitarists throughout the sixties and seventies. He often played on 3 sessions day. Jim started playing the guitar at 14. At 17 he joined Marty Wilde's backing group 'The Wildcats' who also backed Eddie Cochran on his tour of the UK, during which he died in a motorbike accident. The most popular session guitarists at the time of Big Jim's "three a day period" were John McLaughlin, Joe Morretti, Colin Green and Vic Flick. A little later Jimmy Page and Alan Parker started to be used frequently.

'The Wildcats' left Marty Wilde and became 'The Krewcats' and recorded some great instrumentals like *Trambone* and *Peak Hour*. The Krewcats included Brain "Liquorice" Locking on bass and Brian Bennett on drums both of whom who were in 'The Shadows' later. Big Jim has played and recorded with so many well-known people that it would almost be easier to say whom Big Jim has not played for, than to list the artists that have benefited from his superb guitar playing. In 1969 Jim joined Tom Jones, touring and appearing on many TV shows. Jim left Tom in late 1974 and started a record label with Derek Lawrence, the producer of 'Deep Purple', 'Wishbone Ash' and others. Jim also had a band called 'Tiger' along the way. In 1978 he became part of the 'James Last Orchestra' with whom he spent 9 years. He still plays in the local clubs and pubs covering all types of music.

On the day of Mick Jupp's proposed recording session I was working for my father in his technical bookshop when I received a frantic call from Decca (or someone on their behalf) saying that there were 12 musicians, a producer and an engineer at the studio but no Mick! I reluctantly agreed to go round to his house to see where he was and he was still in bed. He had apparently decided that he did not want to go to the session but had not told Decca. Mick is legendary for his uncompromising attitude. He can be very charming and I count him as one of my oldest friends. However, he is also temperamental and will only do what he wants to, when he wants to. Mick is a very talented singer, musician and songwriter but is quite capable of driving his group members nuts! His oft repeated threat was that he would up sticks and 'go to Carlisle' and in point of fact he now lives in the Lake District (not quite Carlisle but pretty close!) I well remember him shouting at his guitar "Why won't you go in tune?" There is a well known story that Bruce Welch, the superb rhythm guitarist of 'The Shadows' got so hung up about tuning problems that he used to pay John Rostill (their sadly departed bass player) to tune him up so he would not need to worry about it any longer. Of course today's players use electronic tuners without even thinking but it was extremely frustrating to say the least to have an otherwise perfect set ruined by dodgy tuning and it did happen to all groups at some time or another.

Other bands in the Southend area began to record at this time and 'The Paramounts' for example had a hit with a cover of a song by 'The Coasters' (*Poison Ivy)* in 1963. The story is that Gary Brooker phoned Mick Jupp the day before the recording session to ask him for the words. Mick was rather surprised as he had seen 'The Paramounts' play this song many times but Gary then admitted that he only knew one verse! Contrast this with the complex lyrics that Keith Reid writes for 'Procol Harum' and it would appear that Gary's memory has got better as he grew older.

Another Southend band that caught my attention was 'The Whirlwinds' who were the ace cover version band. They could copy any song and make it sound like the original. Their guitarist Bert Pulham was very accomplished and part of 'The Whirlwinds' eventually metamorphosed into 'The Crocheted Doughnut Ring' who later recorded various singles and had a number 2 hit in Japan with their single *Havana Anna.* 'The Whirlwinds' became 'Force Five' and their talented personnel, Ronnie Ghent, Dave Gosling, Dave Skates (RIP), Dave Osbourne and Bert Pulham played at a well-known pub in Leigh (near Southend.) At the same time another band of mine, 'The Fingers', played on the non-'Force Five' nights.

I wanted to widen my experience and went for various auditions including one for 'Robb Storm and the Whispers' where I realised that I had a lot to learn when I heard their polished harmonies and was presented with some chord charts that baffled me at the time. They were tactful and said I had a good high harmony voice but I didn't get the job.

9.
Jess Conrad and Rhet Stoller

One audition that I did pass was to join a new backing group for Jess Conrad. At this time (1965) Jess was already a well-known singer. Conrad had early success as a pop star but went on to become an accomplished actor and has appeared in many films, musicals and TV shows, as well as continuing to present his own cabaret act. Jess started as a repertory actor with the famous 'Charles Danville Company' and played seasons in Barnsley and Derby. Jack Good featured him on TV in the original 'Oh Boy' shows. He recorded various hits on Decca. One of his records *This Pullover* was dubbed Kenny Everett's favourite worst record in 1979. Jess was voted 'England's most popular singer' in the 1961 'New Musical Express' poll. In the early 70's he starred as Jesus in 'Godspell', for which he earned rave reviews and in 'Joseph & The Technicolor Dreamcoat' creating the part of Joseph in the Bill Kenwright production. However, in all honesty he was better at being a good-looking showman than he was at singing. The band was good though and the leader of the group, guitarist Rhet Stoller, had already had some chart success with the theme tune from "Cool For Cats." "Cool For Cats" was a popular record show on the TV at the time. Rhet's recording of the theme tune was *Chariot* and it was a chart hit in 1961. Rhet has backed many stars over the years including: Helen Shapiro, Craig Douglas, Eden Kane, Gene Vincent and

Eddie Cochran. Rhet was a very good guitarist and also played glockenspiel. He is alleged to have been the very first guitarist in the UK to use echo on his guitar. He experimented with echo and other effects and also with double tracking way before other musicians in the UK. Rhet was also keen to learn more about the technical aspects of arranging. He played a Burns guitar at the time and it was an unfashionable and bilious green colour. Our first practices were at his house in Stamford Hill in the basement where he introduced me to Bernie Martin who had played drums with him in 'Russ Sainty and the Echoes', a band which Rhet had joined in the very early sixties. (This group evolved into 'Russ Sainty and The Nu-Notes' and was frequently on the radio on programmes like "Saturday Club" and "Easy Beat.")

Rhet's most famous (and probably most lucrative) offering was the theme tune to *Match Of The Day*. He wrote this tune in 1972. I knew another guitarist, Bob Heath, who was inveigled into joining 'The Rhet Stoller Group' and we then learnt Jess Conrad's cabaret repertoire as well as a supporting set for us. Moving from the gritty repertoire of 'The Orioles' to the heady delights of Jess' chosen numbers like *Oh You Beautiful Doll* and *Bye Bye Birdie* made me realise that whilst the experience was valuable the numbers we played were suspect. We did however have some fun in our own supporting sets playing stuff like *Caravan* and Bob (who has a very good voice) sang numbers like *It's Not Unusual*. One night we were playing in a tough Northern Club and a gent stood next to me in the urinal. "Not a bad band son. You should get rid of that poncy singer though," he said. I didn't relay that advice to Jess but it was musically sound. We played twice and sometimes three times a night. The venues were dance halls like 'The Pasadena' or 'The Top Twenty' or nightclubs for the second or third gigs of the day. These bookings were in exotically named places like Scawthorpe, Buttershaw, Kettlethorpe, Batley and Liversedge. I remember one venue vividly. This was 'The Windmill', which was a nightclub in Leeds (or somewhere near like Pudsey!) We shared a dressing room with an "exotic dancer" named Marguerite, who took all her clothes off and proceeded to sprinkle sequins on herself, before going on stage. This was quite an eyeful for a young and sexually inexperienced bass player! There was also a comic called Tony Heath on this show. A very attractive girl singer called Carol Elvin (billed as "Sexy Xy") was also performing at 'The Windmill.' Carol sometimes turns up on compilations like *Dreambabes Vol 2 – Reflections* (RPM Records.) Another nightclub that we played at was 'The Garden of Eden Club' in Manchester where you appeared on a floor surrounded by a four-foot sunken rockery complete with live alligators. Some of Jess' pals turned up one night and he chatted happily to Charles Hawtrey (RIP) (of the "Carry On" films) and also Roy Kinnear (who has also now passed away.) Jess had other commitments and the band work dried up but we did some variety shows at places like 'The Esplanade Theatre' – Bognor Regis where we supported by John McIvor "The Renowned Scottish Tenor" in August 1965. This was one of a series of shows at the Theatre and on other Sundays the shows included Bill Maynard, Dick Emery, Mike Yarwood and 'The Dallas Boys', all very famous acts of the time. One night we finished our act and Jess started to berate me for 'playing in the wrong key' during the introduction to an Anthony Newley song *Do You Mind?* Now what had really happened was that I had played the bass intro (in the right key) and then Jess had started to sing the song off key. I was young and arrogant (like most teenagers) and I argued with him and probably threw in a few swear words. Rhet Stoller took me to one side and gave me some valuable advice. He said even if I was right it was Jess that was paying me. Tact and diplomacy were never my strong points as a youngster but looking back I now realise that Rhet was right. Jess was not really interested in the band as a going concern and even forgot names of the group members at times. One night he introduced Bob and myself to the audience as Bill and Ben. Nobody is all bad and Jess could be very charming even if he was his own greatest fan. One night he treated us to dinner in a club with his then wife who had become famous as the girl in the Camay adverts. ("You'll be a little lovelier each day...") and yes she was lovely although whether or not it was all down to Camay I couldn't really say. The DJ at the club that night was the only person who I have ever met called Garth. He was a Bradford based guy called Garth Cawood. We carried on playing with Jess for some time on and off but I knew that I wanted to join a more modern band and to play more regularly. This was when I heard of an upcoming vacancy in a band called 'The Fingers' who also backed a very attractive young girl singer named Antoinette.

10.
Antoinette and The Fingers

Antoinette (Marie Antoinette Daly) issued her debut record for Decca in 1963. At this time she was only 13 but *Jenny Let Him Go* was a grown up Spectorish sounding record. Unfortunately it was not successful and Decca dropped her. She then recorded five singles for Pye, before moving to the Columbia label in 1966, where she recorded as Toni Daly. 'The Fingers' were her backing band at the time but never issued any records with her. They were a solid, tight band that played a mixed repertoire of songs including numbers by 'The Kinks', 'The Moody Blues' and 'The Beach Boys.' They had already begun to experiment with harmonies and it was then that I realised that I wanted to be a part of this group. Their original bass player, Mike Tew, had decided to join the Army and when he left them I became their new recruit. I bought his 'Fender Precision' from him a little later but at that time I couldn't get on with the longer scale and the very different sound to the 'Epiphone Rivoli' that I have been using and I sold it on to George Bird (who will feature later in this story.) The 'Rivoli' was a reasonably popular bass at the time and my model was the same as the one used by Chas Chandler in 'The Animals.'

At this time I was using what seems like a very low powered amp nowadays but it had a surprisingly good sound. This was a Selmer "Treble and Bass 50" which I was using with a huge Selmer "Goliath" speaker cabinet. The 'Treble and Bass 50' was also a very tough little amp. One day whilst unloading the group van it fell out and hit the street at a rapid rate of knots. One by one the sides unfolded, almost in slow motion, until the innards were exposed for all to see. We nailed the sides back on to each other (and the top) and it worked well for a long time afterwards. 'Selmer' was an old established company formed by Ben Davis and Henri Selmer, with their first UK premises in Moor Street in London. They very soon moved to Charing Cross Road, which was the head office and showroom until the 1970's. 'Selmer' in London was a major importer of brass and woodwind instruments from 'Selmer' in Paris but they had their own brands too. The amplifiers that they made in the sixties were in direct competition with the famous 'Vox' brand. 'Selmer UK' also imported guitars made by 'Hofner', 'Fender' and 'Gibson.' One of the famous budget guitars was the 'Hofner Futurama' that was actually made in the Czech Republic. 'Selmer London' was sold to 'Norlin USA' in the 80's.

The equipment that is available to musicians now is more reliable and sometimes much smaller as the efficiency of amps and speakers has increased considerably in the last 40 years. The funny thing is though is that many musicians still try to get the old sound that they used in the sixties and lots of equipment is badged or sold as the way to achieve that "vintage" sound. My 'Treble and Bass 50' had an awful 'middle' sound so I always turned the knob right off, as I hated the honky middle frequencies. Many of the amps that are sold now have 'presets' that shape the sound and one of the most popular is the so called 'smile' sound that slightly boosts the bass and treble frequencies and cuts the middle which is exactly what I was doing in the early sixties.

One advantage of being in 'The Fingers' was being near the delicious Antoinette. I had the hugest huge crush on Antoinette and was very jealous of all her boy friends. Antoinette and Ricky Mills (the lead guitarist and vocalist of 'The Fingers') went out with each other for some time. I never told Antoinette (or Toni as we knew her) of my not very secret passion at the time but I collected pictures of her for my own benefit. I wasn't a stalker though! At this time we wore turquoise waistcoats with black trimmings and epaulettes. Antoinette's mother, Peggy, made these for us. Peggy was a great character and would pepper her speech with 'Feck this' and 'Feck that' which she maintained was not real swearing. I wasn't too sure that she was right but I understand now that this word can indeed be used in exactly the same way as its more vulgar cousin and that it generally expresses the same emotions. The word is spelt feic in Gaelic, which is similar to the Gaelic verb to look or to see. I used to go to see Peggy for coffee and tomato and onion sandwiches and she always made me very welcome. In fact I visited her so much that my Mum said jokingly that she wondered if I was more interested in Peggy than Antoinette! One person who did not extend a friendly welcome to me was the father of one of Antoinette's friends. I had asked her pal Janet Thorpe to go to the pictures with me and she had agreed. I rang the doorbell of her parents' flat on the evening in question and Janet's father came to the door in a fierce temper. He told me to bugger off or he would throw me over the outside balcony. Janet came to the door behind her father and told me to go to 'Tonnete's' place to wait for her. I was happy to get away from her Dad but to this day I don't know why he was so upset about the idea of me taking Janet to the flicks.

We played at clubs, dance halls and for social functions. One of the places that we played at was a dance hall at the back of a pub called 'The Halfway House' which was where I first saw 'The Whirlwinds' after being nagged by my then girlfriend to do something different rather than just going to coffee bars or the pictures. I was gobsmacked when I saw Ronnie and the other boys with real 'Fender' guitars although Bert used a 'Jazzmaster' rather than the usual 'Strat.'

One day Ricky, Dave and I decided to repaint our group van. Rather than paint it all one boring colour we decided to paint the van black and white and then for the black panels to have white hands on them, whilst the white panels would have black hands emblazoned thereon. The easiest but messiest way to do this was to have trays of paint into which we dipped our hands and then smartly pressed them onto the coachwork. This van was a well-known sight in Southend in those days and you could always see when 'The Fingers' were in town. Ricky and Toni worked well together on stage but as is often the case their off stage relationship sometimes had an effect upon their on stage persona. Eventually they split up and she left the band. She continued to sing as Toni Baxter and has been happily married to Kenny Baxter (a well known Southend jazz saxophonist for many years.) The line up of 'The Fingers' when I joined them was: Rick Mills (lead guitar/vocals) Jim Spicer (drums), Dave Grout (rhythm guitar/vocals) and me on bass/ vocals. We played at many venues in pubs, dance halls and clubs and for functions. One club had a very precious gay manager who used to fancy Ricky and who would give advice about the next number so that we had to contend with him saying: "Ricky, I think we need a nice slow one now..." or "Ricky, I do think a nice fast one would be good next..." Needless to say, his admiration of Ricky was not returned! Our manager was a friendly guy who had a car tire shop in Leigh, near Southend - Dick Mountney. Dick also managed 'Force Five' and did his best to get us work and a recording contract. He also arranged other work for us out of town and I recall playing in Margate one night supporting 'Sounds Incorporated', who were a very fine instrumental band with a super but conceited drummer called Tony Newman. Tony Newnan made a point of belittling our efforts but luckily we knew that we had a band that we liked and so his comments did not permanently dent our self-confidence.

'Sounds Incorporated' was a six-man band and first got together in 1961. The line up was: Dave Glyde (tenor, soprano, flute & clarinet), Alan Holmes (tenor baritone, flute, alto flute, oboe & cor anglais), Baz Elmes (baritone, organ & piano), John Gillard (guitar) Dick Thomas (bass guitar) and the aforementioned Tony Newman (drums and big head.) 'Sounds Incorporated' were offered a tour backing Gene Vincent early on in their life and they quickly became THE band which provided backing for visiting artists from the States. They backed many of these artists and the big American names with whom they appeared included; Gene Vincent, Jerry Lee Lewis, Little Richard, Sam Cooke, Ben E. King, Brenda Lee, Mary Wells, The Shirelles, Eddie Floyd, Freddie Cannon, Gene Pitney, Jose Feliciano, and Big Dee Irwin. They also backed many UK artists. 'The Beatles' manager Brian Epstein took on Sounds Incorporated in 1963 and they then started to back Cilla Black. They were also good friends with 'The Beatles' from experiences in Germany and supported the Fab Four on many occasions both here and abroad. By 1967 Tony Newman had left to become a session player career and was replaced by Terry Fogg. Later in '67 Baz left and was replaced by Trevor White who was a great singer. The band was changing style and now became a cabaret act. 'Sounds Incorporated' recorded many tunes and their version of *The William Tell Overture* was number 1 hit in Australia. Finally In 1969 they split up.

11.
The Elms

The most popular dance hall in the Southend area at that time was at the back of 'The Elm Hotel' (always known as 'The Elms.') The aforementioned 'Force Five' played several times a week and another band, 'The Monotones' appeared on the other nights.

'Force Five' were a very good covers band with an exceptional guitarist in Bert Pulham. The other members were: Ronnie Gent (who was their lead vocalist and with whom I was in a band called 'King Kong' some years later), Pete Gosling, (rhythm), Dave (Oz) Osbourne, (bass), and Dave Skates (drums). They released five singles between 1964 and 1966 (including the excellent *Yeah, I'm Waiting*.) These 45's were all issued on the United Artists label. The band was formed in 1960 and was allegedly called 'The Shadows' at first. They changed their name to 'The Whirlwinds' and later they became 'Force Five.' George Bird played bass for them later as well as singing lead on some of their singles e.g. *Don't Know Which Way To Turn*.

'The Monotones' (whose leader was Brian Alexander), issued four singles on Pye in 1965 and 1965. They later evolved into 'The Treetops', a good harmony band in which Brian was also the lead guitarist. When 'The Monotones' decided to leave to play at a Mecca venue elsewhere the landlord of 'The Elms' formed his own replacement group. Although he did not personally play in the band he thought that by selecting the right musicians and putting them together he would have an instant success and a loyal band that would play at the pub for a long time to come. Unfortunately for them and him too, the band folded but fortunately for 'The Fingers', Dick Mountney persuaded the landlord to take them on to replace them. There was one proviso; we had to let the organist of the old band join us. We heard him play and he was much better than we thought he would be. This organist was Alan Beecham and he was a jazzer at heart but at least this meant that his knowledge of chords was very useful and he was a laid back, friendly kind of guy too. He had a deceptively quiet sense of humour and was an artist too. I remember one of his efforts that had Smarties stuck all over it. Now if this had been entered for the Turner prize I am sure it would have been an instant success. There were some real characters at 'The Elms.' Lionel was the doorman and he was about five feet wide and it was all muscle. Luckily he was the archetypal gentle giant but he was very useful whenever a fight started. Tubby was the cellar man and his method of moving a steel barrel was to put it on the floor and to roll it along kicking it in the right direction. Not long after we started playing at 'The Elms', Jim our drummer decided to leave and we turned to Bob Clouter the ex-Oriole to replace him. 'The Fingers' were very popular locally and we were beginning to experiment with different numbers rather than playing the usual chart covers. We rehearsed at 'The Elms' and we were merciless with ourselves. We would frequently spend all day on one song, going over the arrangement and the harmonies, until we were satisfied that we were doing the song justice. I am afraid I used to take myself a little too seriously in those days and would get quite bossy. (What's that you are saying – "Arrogant git"?) I did not have much sympathy for mistakes or latecomers to these rehearsals and I remember berating Dave one day until he said; "OK I'm sorry I was late but I fell asleep on the pavement and only just woke up!"

At about that time The Rolling Stones confused everybody by using a fuzz box on *Satisfaction*. Where was the sax player? How did they manage to get that sound with a guitar? We turned to our old mate Lefty and asked him to build a fuzz box for Ricky. Today's audiences are used to multi-effects and even digitally modelled simulations of certain amp and speaker combinations. The effects available in the early to middle sixties were limited. If you had a "Watkins Copicat" Echo Unit you were lucky. This used tapes to provide limited variations of reverb and echo and when you could not buy replacement tapes (or could not afford them) you used Sellotape to join the old broken ones. This had the unfortunate side effect of producing an audible blip every time the join ran through the heads. If you were very, very lucky you had something like a "Binson Echorec", which used a disc to produce the echo effects. Binson echo units were first made in the late1950's. Echo effects were comparatively primitive at the time but the Binson was the crème de la crème.

The discs in Binson units allegedly have a life of 40+ years so compared to the fragile tapes in the Copicat this was obviously a good prospect. The Echorecs were also quieter in operation but they were expensive. But back to the Lefty made fuzz box, this produced lovely farting guitar distortion and Ricky used and over used this in many numbers like *Hold on I'm Coming*. 'The Fingers' went for an audition at 'Aeolian Hall' for the BBC and when Ricky used the fuzz box the technicians ran in to the room and asked him what he was using and how it worked. We passed the audition and then waited hopefully for some radio work.

Ricky was also changing and he was becoming a much

more dynamic showman. He really could make any audience eat out of the palm of his hand. After some time we had a council of war (without Ricky) and decided that we would like to bring in another ex-Oriole, Mo (Maurice) Witham so that Ricky could leave the lead guitar duties to him and concentrate on singing and his new found talent of making the punters happy via his very energetic showmanship. I remember playing songs like *But I was Cool* by Oscar Brown Jr. where Ricky would fall to his knees groaning and crying during crucial parts of this very strange song. I saw Rolf Harris do the same song on TV much later and he implied that he had written it especially for the show. I wrote and complained about this distortion of the truth and was told that he was just using poetic licence to improve his show (or words to the same effect.)

By recruiting Mo we now had four singers. Ricky was always our main lead singer but with four of us able to sing we began to experiment with four part harmonies (sixths and ninths etc), falsetto tracked with the same notes an octave down and passing harmonies. Our practice routines became even lengthier but we felt that the extra work was creating a significant improvement to the overall sound of the band. Alan was also helping the new line up to expand our repertoire by contributing jazzy versions of tunes like *A Taste of Honey* and we included various soul and Tamla Motown songs too. (Alan used to write jazzy tunes too. I recall that he used to play one named *Pigostrophe* when he was in his earlier band 'The Milestones.') Alan played a "Vox Continental" organ when we met him. The "Vox Continental" started life in the early 1960s. I understand that it was probably the first organ created specifically for professional stage use. It was made by the Jennings Organ Company who also built church organs & the Vox amps used by both 'The Shadows' and 'The Beatles.' The 'Continental' had a 4-octave keyboard and six drawbars, which were used for tone setting. This organ was marginally better than the dreaded "Farfisa" organ used by some bands. However, it still couldn't produce the rich and varied tones of the "Hammond" organ. The Hammond organ is still the favourite sound of many keyboard players and famous Hammond players have included Jimmy Smith, Jimmy McGriff, Booker T and Matthew Fisher. Like Gary Brooker when he was in 'The Paramounts', Alan also acquired a "Hohner Pianet." This electric piano was first made in 1962. The "Hohner Pianet" needed to be played hard but it was light in weight. The Pianet had quite a good sound for its time but didn't sound very much like a piano at all. The Pianet sound is more familiar than you might think as it was used on some very well known records like: *My Best Friend* (Queen), *She's Not There* (The Zombies) and *Joy To The World* (Three Dog Night.) I recall talking to Gary Brooker shortly after he got his Pianet and complimenting him on the sound of his new organ. He surprised me by telling me that it was an electric piano. The Hammond is still THE organ and used with the famous "Leslie" Cabinet it can produce the most wonderful sounds, including the famous swelling organ. (Of course swelling organs have got a lot of musicians into trouble.) The Leslie Rotating Speaker was named after its inventor, Don Leslie. When used with a Hammond the pairing is as perfect as Bacon and Eggs, Laurel and Hardy or Lennon and McCartney. The Leslie operates on what is apparently a simple principle; a directional sound source rotates at constant (or variable) speed around a fixed pivot point. OK so you need to hear it to understand how great it sounds!

I also remember feeble attempts by 'The Fingers' to get some newspaper coverage by visiting top hotels with an eight-foot hand. At the first salubrious establishment the staff totally ignored the huge hand so we tried to enter 'The Hilton' in London. They were much more reluctant to let us sully their premises with our massive wooden hand and promptly threw us out. We still didn't get much press coverage though, except for some small mentions in magazines like 'Princess' (for young girls, who probably couldn't even afford to buy records.)

The Fingers on Westcliff beach – 1966 (L to R)
Dave Grout, Bob Clouter, John Bobin (Top layer!)
Alan Beecham, Ricky Mills (Bottom layer!)

This was before groups started destroying gear and TV's on stage and wrecking hotel rooms. We were pretty tame compared to 'The Who' or 'The Move' but we couldn't afford to replace dead and damaged guitars and speakers at the rate they did. We did invent a fake history for the band that seemed to be more interesting than fact. The idea was that we had all played together in a Symphony Orchestra lead by the world famous (and also fictitious) 'Earl Sims'. Finding the classics to be too tame we had made the quantum leap to pop. I'm sure nobody believed the story even then.

We played as the supporting act to many famous sixties artists such as 'Cliff Bennett and the Rebel Rousers' who had a large (by those days' standards) line up with a good brass section. Cliff Bennett sang in a 'Vertigo' act later, which was called 'Toe Fat.' (Vertigo was a label owned by 'Philips' that had an impressive roster of talent on its books. One of my later bands, 'Legend' recorded for Vertigo and our 'dizzy' spell is described later.) 'Toe Fat' were infamous for shooting out the windscreens of following cars and vans with an air pistol. Before I get sued for repeating this story let me tell you I haven't got the faintest idea if it is true or not but it was an oft told tale in those days. Cliff Bennett (born in 1940) formed the 'Rebel Rousers' in early 1961. The line up was Mick King (lead guitar), Frank Allen (bass), Sid Phillips (piano, saxophone) and Ricky Winters (drums). For a short while Joe Meek looked after the band and they recorded several early but unsuccessful singles with Joe. They recorded some R&B covers with little more success until their winter of 1964 hit *One Way Love.* This was a cover of a song by 'The Drifters.' In the same year Frank Allen left and joined to 'The Searchers.' They next covered another ditty by 'The Drifters' called *I'll Take You Home* but this record failed to dent the Top 30 and only reached no. 43. Brian Epstein's company 'NEMS' took over the band and Paul McCartney produced their version of the Lennon and McCartney song *Got To Get You Into My Life.* This reached number 6 in the charts but was their last Top 10 hit. After a brief spell as 'Cliff Bennett and his Band' and some experimentation with other writers Cliff split the band up in 1969. This was when he formed 'Toe Fat' (mentioned above in respect of their pranks with air rifles.) In 1972, Cliff tried again with a new band called 'Rebellion', and in 1975 he had a band called 'Shanghai'. Despite all his hard work these two bands did not register strongly with the punters. Over the years Cliff's bands issued some sterling work. Cliff Bennett issued five solid albums; various singles and his bands still appear periodically on diverse compilations. Cliff Bennett now works in the advertising business, but still plays semi-professionally.

'Simon Dupree and the Big Sound' was another band that we supported and they had a huge hit with *Kites*. They also later formed the basis of 'Gentle Giant'; another 'Vertigo' band. The band (from Portsmouth) was first formed by three talented brothers; Derek, Ray and Phil Shulman. Derek sang lead vocals, Ray played lead guitar and Phil was a saxist and trumpeter. At one time the brothers Shulman had a band called 'The Howlin' Wolves' and they also used the name 'The Roadrunners.' In 1966 they adopted the new name 'Simon Dupree and The Big Sound.' Eric Hine (keyboards), Pete O'Flaherty (bass) and Tony Ransley (drums) were also in the group and they were popular on the soul and R&B club circuit. Three of their singles; *I See The Light"*, *"Reservations"* and *"Daytime Nightime"* were radio hits and floor fillers at the clubs. An album *Without Reservations*, was issued in 1967 and then they transmutated into flower power in the same year with their huge hit *Kites* which got to no. 9 even though the band were not fond of the record. Later singles were not so successful but they issued a cult classic called *We Are The Moles*, as 'The Moles' in 1969. The band split up in 1969 when Derek Shulman had a nervous breakdown. When he recovered he and his brothers became the bedrock for the progressive band 'Gentle Giant.'

12.
The Cliffs Pavilion

Another place that we played at very regularly at about this time was 'The Cliffs Pavilion.' One night at 'The Cliffs' (in Westcliff on Sea) we played with two other bands, called 'Mooche' and 'The Flies.'

'Mooche' had Jeff Dann on drums, Ian Pearce on lead guitar, Dave Soars on bass, Spud Tatum on organ and lead vocals and Dave Winthrope on sax. They released one single on Pye and this 45 was called, *Hot Smoke And Sassafras*. Mooche came from Chelmsford/Sudbury. Dave Winthrope later joined 'Supertramp.'

'The Flies' were a Psychedelic band that recorded three singles in 1966, 1967 and 1968. The first one was a version of a B-side by 'The Monkees.' *I'm Not Your Stepping Stone* was released on 'Decca' (as was the second single, although their third 45 came out on the 'RCA' label.) They had an outrageous stage act that involved face painting and palm leaf skirts.

At about this time 'The Fingers' were working through an agency called 'The Phillip Birch Agency.' They had a wide range of artists on their books such as:

- 'The Style'
- Jon
- Jackie Edwards (a great singer who also wrote *Keep On Running* which was a huge hit for 'The Spencer Davis Group')

- 'Episode Six' (whose members included Roger Glover and Ian Gillan pre-'Deep Purple')
- 'The Symbols'
- 'The Smoke'

13.
Peter Eden

Asingular influence on 'The Fingers' came about via our introduction to Peter Eden. Peter had been a co-manager of Donovan with the well-known songwriter Geoff Stephens, after hearing Donovan support the R&B band 'Cops and Robbers' at a live gig in Southend in 1964.

Over the years Pete has played a part in records by artists as diverse as John Surman, G T Moore, 'The Crocheted Doughnut Ring', Barry Fantoni and Bill Fay. You can see from this list that Pete has no fixed ideas about the music with which he becomes involved and his talent is to sprinkle unusual ideas onto the artists and songs that he produces. A recent limited edition vinyl compilation called *Nice* was issued on Tenth Planet records and it is a good introduction to Pete's work. This features some previously unissued Fingers tracks, which were recorded in the sixties.

- *Look Away* was recorded at 'Maximum Sound' in Dean Street by an early version of 'The Fingers' circa 1964. It was unreleased until it was featured on *Nice*.
- *It's Just Like Loving You Baby* and *I Hear The Sun* were recorded at the 'EMI' studio in Abbey Road in June 1967. These were both unreleased until they were featured on *Nice*.
- *I Go to Sleep* (more details later!) and *Oh* (recorded at

the same session as *Look Away*) were released in 1966. *Oh* was also laid down at the 'Maximum Sound' session.

Dick Mountney suggested to us that the band needed some artistic advice regarding our repertoire and our stage act and after talking to Peter we agreed to take him on as an additional 'artistic adviser.' Pete had a totally different idea of what we should play, what we should wear and how we should publicise the band to the one that we had. The first thing Pete did was to radically change our repertoire by persuading us that the emerging west coast 'Greenwhich Village' acts were more credible than the soul and pop repertoire that we had built up. The new influences were many and varied but the favourites were 'The Young Rascals', 'The Loving Spoonful' and other acts such as Timi Hardin plus some minor artists like 'The Trade Winds.' We experimented with different instruments like autoharps and mellotrons both of which we used in later recording sessions. Autoharps play chords and sound like a shimmery, silvery harp but you can get this sound without being an expert. By pressing keys down with one hand and strumming the strings you can achieve a very acceptable sound right off. You do need to know the chord names even if you don't know how to form them on a traditional instrument like a guitar, say. There are 15 and 21 chord versions but I cannot recall which one Ricky used to use. Mellotrons were a daft idea. They used tapes of real instruments like violins and were extremely temperamental. Not only that the whole thing was the size of a "Hammond" Organ so transport was always a problem. The one that we experimented with was at the 'Abbey Road' studios.

We had dressed like any other group until now and the then current phase was anything bright and colourful. We used dye our own shirts and the results were not too bad if I say so myself. We had also been through the usual 'Beatles' look and now wanted to be different. We were promptly geared up with Grandad vests (well in advance of the coming trend), large hillbilly hats and wide braces. This quasi-country yokel look lasted for some time and in truth we did get noticed for it. One of the other local bands ('The Spooks') copied the look until we told them off! I suppose we should have realised that imitation is the sincerest form of flattery. The band was itching to get onto the recording studio. An earlier self-financed session at 'Maximum Sound' had resulted in us laying down a Geoff Stephens track *Can't Live it Down* and some covers like *Look Away* (later released on the vinyl only limited edition of Peter Eden productions called *Nice* – see above) and also *Something You Got*. (*Something You Got* is still unreleased.) Vic Keary set up 'Maximum Sound.' This studio was in the West End of London but moved later to The Old Kent Road. Manfred Mann eventually bought 'Maximum Sound.' He also changed its name to 'The Workhouse.'

David Wells of 'Tenth Planet Records' (who has a huge knowledge of the era, the music and the records that were released in the sixties) compiled the anthology, *Nice*. 'Tenth Planet' is now one of the leading reissue labels around and specialises in Vinyl, although it now has a CD offshoot called 'Wooden Hill.' It was started in the early 1990's to help collectors and 60's/early 70's fans as their favourite genre was becoming harder and harder to source. The idea was that all releases would be in a limited edition format and the label has put out many previously unreleased or very rare tracks.

14.

Polydor

The Fingers' were no nearer to getting that vital record deal but 'Force Five' were already old hands and they had recorded a Ray Davies number called *I Go to Sleep* (later – much later – a hit for 'The Pretenders.') The backing track was great but the record company was not happy with the vocals so Pete suggested that we should take the recording and add our vocals. We were unhappy about this as we wanted to play on our own record but we were offered a small sop in that a number written by Ricky and me; *Oh* would be the B-side. *Oh* had already been recorded during the session that produced *Can't Live it Down* and featured an autoharp on a simple early 'Beatles' type number. (As mentioned above *Oh* also appeared on the Peter Eden anthology *Nice*.)

We trouped off to add our vocals and the end result was a pleasant but unremarkable version of Ray's number. *I Go to Sleep* was released on 'Polydor' in 1966. 'Disc and Music Echo' had this to say about the record:

"The best version I've heard of *I Go To Sleep* pops up by The Fingers."

When we met Ray Davies whilst we were supporting 'The Kinks' later on in Ramsgate, he remembered that we had recorded this song but he didn't comment on our version.

'The Kinks', led by Ray Davies, had their finest hour with *You Really Got Me*. Their initial line up had Mick Avory on drums, Ray's brother Dave on lead guitar and occasional lead vocals, Ray himself on rhythm and lead vocals and Pete Quaife on bass. In 1963 Ray met Alexis Korner (a hugely influential UK Bluesman) and this led to Ray and Dave working on the new London R&B circuit with a band called 'The Ravens' (and in a blues outfit called 'The Dave Hunt Band.') 'The Ravens' became 'The Kinks' in 1963 when Mick Avory joined as drummer. Their first 45, was a cover of *Long Tall Sally* but it flopped and this was also the fate of the follow-up, *You Still Want Me*, written by Ray Davies. Then came the great *You Really Got Me*, which made number 1 here and number 7 in the USA in 1964. They also issued their first album at this stage which made number 3 in the UK. The follow-up to *You Really Got Me* was *All Day And All Of The Night,* and this was another massive smash hit (No 2 UK, No 7 US). The single *Tired Of Waiting* (No 1 UK, No 6 US) came next and showed Ray's writing in a different and more laconic vein. Another album reached number three but was less successful in the States. Over the years they have been tremendously prolific and Ray has written several pop operas. *Lola* reached number 2 here (a story about a visitor to a club picking up a lovely girl who turned out to be a transvestite) and reenergised fortunes of 'The Kinks' in 1970. They are still a well-respected band and Ray has been touring recently with an acoustic set. Like most long lasting bands there have been various personnel changes. Bob Henrit and Jim Rodford now play with The Kinks. (Both were once with 'Argent.') Their keyboard player, Ian Gibbons, joined them in 1979 and is also a Southend guy. He has played with many people including 'Dr Feelgood.' Coincidentally Ian was once a member of a band called 'Life', which was the title of the first of two 'Legend' singles on which I played bass. Ian was also a member of another band called 'English Assassins', which featured Nigel Benjamin (who later joined 'Mott the Hoople') and Phil Mitchell who played bass in 'Legend' after I left them and who is now a 'Dr Feelgood' long-term stalwart.

One memorable evening was the 'Melody Maker National Beat Contest' where we were "guest stars" and we had to mime to *I Go To Sleep* in front of 2,000 people. This contest was hosted by Barry Kingston (a 'Top Rank' DJ) and Emperor Rosko (from 'Radio Caroline.')

'The Fingers' also wanted to be on the radio and as we had passed our BBC audition we hoped that the release of *I Go to Sleep* would get us airplay. We had many plays on pirate radio stations like 'Radio Caroline' and 'Radio London.' For example we appeared on the 'Big L' playlist in October 1966 with *I'll Take You Where The Music's Playing.* One of the Radio London DJ's (Keith Skues) had chosen this record as his climber but if failed to dent the Radio London chart. We did however; get to no. 32 with *All Kinds Of People* and this single can now cost up to £50 to get hold of. Ricky Mills (backed by 'The Fingers') appeared in the 'Radio London' chart a few months later as 'Daddy Lindberg.' (*Shirl*, was the record in question.)

When we played at 'High Wycombe College', in December 1966 we were inducted into 'The Knees Club.' We were apparently "the last, and probably the least-known group to join the Knees Club." Mary Wingert founded 'The Knees Club' and the club had its own journal ('Knees Monthly.') This was a stencilled labour of love (no photocopiers then!) and Mary would sign each copy as 'Editor and Founder Member.' 'The Knees Club' had some interesting members such as: 'The Merseys' and Jeff Beck (who was in 'The Yardbirds' at the time.) Ian Gillan and Roger Glover (then in 'Episode Six'), Rod Evans and Ian Paice, (from the group 'M15', (later called 'The Maze') Ritchie Blackmore ('Neil Christian and The Crusaders') were all 'Knees Club' members so Mary had a full 'Deep Purple' contingent. Ray Ennis of 'The Swinging Blue Jeans' even asked if he could be the club's vice-president! The most well known member was David Bowie.

We became chart climbers for other stations too and then our records became hits in some of the other pirate radio charts. Now this doesn't mean that they were hits in official charts but it did get us some interest from fans and the press. Coincidentally companies owned by the radio stations sometimes published our B-sides. (Isn't that spooky?)

15.
Columbia

The Fingers wanted to record a song that we were already playing in our stage act and in 1966 Peter agreed that we could try out *I'll Take You Where The Music's Playing.* This song was popular when we played live but again we were told that we could sing on the record but that this time very well known session musicians would provide the backing. The lead guitarist was Alan Parker (later with 'Blue Mink') and Joe Morretti supplied the rhythm guitar.

Alan Parker was one of the most highly respected session guitarists of the time and has played on many hits. He has worked with artists such as Donovan, Elton John, 'CCS' and 'The Strawbs.' Alan has also contributed huge volumes of work to music libraries in the 1960's to 1980's. He was a founder member of the successful chart act 'Blue Mink' in the late sixties and early seventies and was also in another successful hit band 'The Congregation.' Alan has also worked extensively on TV music for programmes such as 'Van der Valk' and 'Minder.' He has also provided music for films such as 'Jaws 3.' He is a talented arranger and has worked with artists like Dusty Springfield, 'The Walker Brothers' and John Denver.

Joe Morretti was another old-stager and he had played the famous riff in *Shakin' All Over*, possibly the greatest English Rock and Roll number, by 'Johnny Kidd and the Pirates.' A later story has it that Joe was actually the guitarist on the Jet Harris records *Scarlett O'Hara* and *Applejack.*

The pianist was a wild chap named Nicky Hopkins who recorded with many acts from the late sixties over a crucial period of two decades. He has played with many diverse acts such as 'The Rolling Stones', 'The Beatles', 'The Kinks', 'The Who', 'The Jeff Beck Group', 'The Steve Miller Band' and 'Jefferson Airplane'. He was an early member of Screaming Lord Sutch's band but he much preferred recording to touring. He only recorded three solo albums but I bet you have him in your record collection somewhere! He died in October 1994 (RIP.)

But that isn't all – our drummer for this session was Clem Cattini, the well-known musician from 'The Tornados.' Clem's session history is long and very well documented elsewhere but just some of the artists that have been lucky enough to use his drumming skills are Mike Batt, Mike Berry. Phil Everly 'Johnny Kidd & The Pirates', Hank Marvin, P.J.Proby and Lou Reed.

We were disappointed not to appear on 'our' record but we had to admit that the replacements were pretty good by any standards. The backing track did have to be recorded several times and after one take, one of the brass section members was holding his top lip and talking at the same time to Pete. (Try it and you will see that it becomes quite difficult to hear what is being said.) It transpired that this gent was complaining that he had a sore lip. He was saying: "It's only a bit of flesh you know!"

The B-side was a Geoff Stephens song called *My Way Of Thinking*. The many worthies mentioned above recorded the backing track for this song. However, when we went to add our vocals we found that the track was too high for Ricky. Pete said this was no problem and he suggested that we should slow it down so Ricky could add the vocals in a lower key. He said he would then speed it up again. Unfortunately this had a strange effect on the sound of the lead vocal and Ricky sounds as if he is attempting a squeaky Buddy Holly impersonation. The A side was good but Pete didn't like the lead guitar fills that Alan Parker had played in between the vocal lines. These fills were very good and great playing in our opinion but Pete asked Mo to overdub a very simple riff in all the old familiar places.

A 'New Musical Express' reviewer commented on *I'll Take You Where The Music's Playing* in October 1966: "The Fingers version of the Greenwich-Barry number *I'll Take You Where The Music's Playing* is noteworthy for its fund of colourful sounds and ideas."

'The Fingers' recorded at Abbey Road (except for *I Go To Sleep* and the *Can't Live It Down* session both of which were recorded in 1966), and it was inspiring to be where so many big acts had recorded. Many well known artists have recorded at 'Abbey Road', such as some of the classical greats and very famous pop and rock acts including: Eric Clapton, 'Pink Floyd', Gene Pitney, 'Procol Harum', 'Oasis', Sting, Kate Bush, Sir Cliff Richard, 'The Spice Girls', John Lennon and Yoko Ono and, of course, 'The Beatles.'

Sir Edward Elgar conducted the first ever recording session at the HMV Studio as it was called then. 'The London Symphony Orchestra' recorded *Land of Hope and Glory* at this session. Glenn Miller also recorded his last tracks there in 1944. The first major pop star to record there was Cliff Richard with his band 'The Drifters', (who became 'The Shadows.')

Sir George Martin started working at 'Abbey Road' in 1950 when he ran the classical section of Parlophone. 'The Beatles' auditioned for George Martin in 1962 after having been turned down by 'Decca.' 'The Hollies' also recorded at

'Abbey Road', as did 'Pink Floyd' and (surprise surprise!) Cilla Black.

One day 'The Fingers' noticed a big stack of guitar cases in the corner about six feet high. These were guitars left there by 'The Beatles' and we quickly looked through the contents and tried out guitars that tickled our fancy.

One thing that didn't tickle our fancy was the 'Abbey Road' hamburger. After hours there was a coin machine that would deliver a hot but very soggy hamburger, which would fill a hole but was not exactly the kind of food that the truckers would have appreciated. The best places to eat whilst on the road back then were the places that lorry drivers went to. The way to judge an establishment's food was to see how many trucks were parked outside. These cafes specialised in fry-ups and the tea was poured into a trayful of cups without stopping, as the trick was to get from cup to cup as fast as possible.

At one of these roadside cafes there were cups full of brown and red sauce, on the tables, one of which Ricky supplemented with a half sucked cough sweet. How thoughtful! At least the truckers would have been able to breathe more easily.

One night we were playing at a place called 'Davey Jones' Locker' in Lowestoft. Ricky had been having some tummy trouble and disappeared into the loo adjoining the tatty dressing room. He reappeared with a natty handkerchief in his top pocket that matched his shirt. He had been stranded in the loo after his big event with no toilet paper. Being an enterprising kind of chap he had torn the tail off his shirt, used half as toilet paper and the other half as the new top pocket handkerchief display.

Another example of his innovative usage of clothes was the underpants theory, which I think (and hope) was said more for effect than as a real strategy to adopt. The theory went like this: Underpants should be worn for at least four weeks before being washed.

- Week 1 the pants are worn the normal way.
- Week 2 they are worn inside out.
- Week 3 they are worn back to font and finally
- Week 4 they are worn inside out and back to front.

I'll Take You Where The Music's Playing flopped but 'Columbia' (our then record company) still wanted to keep trying and we went back to 'Abbey Road' to record the Geoff Stephens song *All Kinds Of People*, issued in 1967. This time we added harpsichord and although we were not fond of the song it still sounds quite fresh even today. The B-side was a song called *Circus With A Female Clown,* which was co-written by Ricky and me, with help from Pete. Pete's song writing credit was listed as 'Ducky' because he did not wish to complicate his relationship with EMI.

In January 1967 the 'Record Retailer & Music Industry News' said this about *All Kinds Of People.* "One of the more way-out British groups but here in a surprisingly restrained mood. Neat vocal harmonies on a strong-sounding song – quite a few gimmicks. But a minor hit at best." *Circus With A Female Clown* has appeared on various Psychedelic compilations such as *Psychedelia At Abbey Road* and *Circus Days Volumes 1 and 2.*

Pete had by now talked us into styling ourselves as one of the very first Psychedelic acts in Britain. We experimented with strange lighting effects that were often built by Ricky from old speaker cabinets and record players, which supplied the moving parts for early strobe effects. We also made up stories for the press such as the fact that we allegedly stabbed a poor teddy bear to death on stage every night and that this wretched stuffed creature was full of lovely spurting tomato ketchup. We also had an entirely imaginary pet monkey that we said produced psychotic smells. These daft tales have resurfaced on the sleeve notes to some of the compilations that have featured 'The Fingers' in the last few years.

Our next recorded effort (again in 1967), was (you guessed it) another Geoff Stephens song called *Shirl*. Now we had used up our allotted recording time for the year so Pete booked us in as 'Daddy Lindberg' and 'The Fingers' provided the backing for Ricky's new persona 'Daddy Lindberg.' *Shirl* featured a 'Salvation Army' bass drum which looked great on stage but which sounded awful on the record. We also used a mellotron that we found in the 'Abbey Road' studio. The mellotron was the keyboard instrument that played tapes of 'real' instruments such as violins. Alan became a string section for that record as well as playing piano. We finished the session with about twenty minutes to spare but had no B-side. Rather than waste the time we wrote and recorded a stomping piece of nonsense called *Wade In The Shade*. (This was in February 1967.) Thirty-six years later this recording was featured on two separate Psychedelic compilations called *We Can Fly Volume 3* (Past and Present Records) and *Papermen Fly in the Sky* (Paper Records.) This is what the sleeve note writers thought of our efforts: "A great stomper which is starting to be recognised for the gem it is." And "Been on the DJ decks for a few years this one, but it's time to nail the beast onto 33 rpm. A smashing Peter Eden produced ditty that dips into Lysergic soup like a loaf of bread. *Shirl* it's commercial flip stinks! & should be scratched from existence." 'Daddy Lindberg' posters of the time showed Ricky in flying goggles and an old raincoat and he used these same goggles (purchased from an 'Army and Navy' surplus store) when his car windscreen (a mini) was smashed until he could afford to replace it.

Geoff Stephens had arranged for his famous song

Winchester Cathedral to be recorded at about this time by some session musicians and vocalist John Carter. (Carter was a great songwriter too and he was also in a duo called 'Carter-Lewis' as well as being in 'The Ivy League' and 'The Flowerpot Men.') *Winchester Cathedral* was issued as being by 'The New Vaudeville Band.' Geoff began writing in the1950's but by 1964 he had his first hit *Tell Me When*, which he wrote with Les Reed and which was a hit for 'The Applejacks'. Also in 1964 he and Peter Eden discovered and managed Donovan. Geoff co-wrote many famous songs but one of the best to my mind was a song that he wrote by himself called *The Crying Game,* which was a big hit for Dave Berry in 1964. This record featured Big Jim Sullivan using a tone and volume pedal to produce the superb crying effect on his guitar.

When *Winchester Cathedral* was a hit he needed a band to become 'The New Vaudeville Band', to tour and record the follow up. Pete asked us if we wanted to be 'The New Vaudeville Band' but we turned this opportunity down. (Apparently this honour was offered to 'The Bonzo Dog Doo-Dah Band' too and they also declined.) However, two of our friends from Southend, Henri Harrison (a former drummer for 'Cops and Robbers') and guitarist Mick Wilsher did grab the opportunity with both hands. *Winchester Cathedral* was followed by other Geoff Stephens penned hits for 'The New Vaudeville Band.' Many other artists such as 'Manfred Mann', 'The Hollies', Tom Jones, Cliff Richard and 'Herman's Hermits' have had hits with Geoff Stephens songs (either written by him alone or co-written with other composers.)

The Fingers continued to support many top acts and I remember one night we played as a warm up act for Long John Baldry (now sadly departed) and his band, 'Bluesology'. This band had a good organist who would later become Elton John.)

Long John Baldry has always had a deep, gruff and throaty blues voice. He also encouraged young fat Reg Dwight to turn himself into old fat Elton John and pushed Rod Stewart into the limelight. In one of his first bands the drummer was Charlie Watts (later drummer of' The Rolling Stones'.) Long John was born in 1941 and his early stint with Cyril Davies won him respect at a young age. When Cyril Davies died he formed 'The Hoochie Coochie Men', which included Rod Stewart. Long John then moved to 'Steam Packet', which also included Rod as well as Brian Auger (demon organist!) and Julie Driscoll. Not long thereafter came the 'Bluesology' period but then Long John started to record more commercial songs. Those songs were not the best representation of his bluesy voice. However, *Let The Heartaches Begin* was a big hit in 1967, a number one in fact, which is more than any of my records have ever been. The Olympic Games' theme *Mexico* followed and that also entered the Top 20 the next year. Unfortunately, the hits dried up and LJB recorded a new album called *It Ain't Easy* with his old pals, Reg and Rod. However, it wasn't easy and it didn't sell. John went to New York and Los Angeles and later he emigrated to Vancouver where he played the club circuit. In the early 90's he played yet another part, as the voice for Sonic the Hedgehog on the computer game. A new Long John Baldry album was released in 1993, which he called *It Still Ain't Easy.*

'The Zombies' was another band that we played with and their singer Colin Blunstone impressed us with his pure, breathy style of singing. 'The Zombies' started life as an R&B group but they gradually acquired their own style. Their most famous song was their first hit *She's Not There* but *Tell Her No* and *Time Of The Season* were also fine songs and were successful for the band. These great songs were all co-written by keyboard player Rod Argent and the bass player, Chris White. The band issued a famous last album called *Odyssey & Oracle*. Their last single, *Imagine The Swan* was a massive five minutes in length. Rod Argent then joined 'Argent' and it was this band that recorded *Hold Your Head Up* a very popular song at the time. The guitarist of Argent was Russ Ballard (whom I had first heard of as a member of 'The Roulettes', when I was in 'The Phantoms.') Collin Blunstone issued several albums in the 70s but these traded heavily on name 'The Zombies' and even their actual songs. Some of 'The Zombies' were featured on the 1990's *Colin Blunstone Sings His Greatest Hits* and two albums were issued in the early '90s that included all the members bar Rod Argent.

In February 1967 'The Fingers' appeared live on a 'BBC Light Programme' radio show called 'Monday Monday' Barry Aldiss was the introducer and we were of course familiar with him because he was a well-known radio DJ of the time having first come to prominence via 'Radio Luxembourg.' The other acts were Julie Felix, and 'Dave Dee, Dozy, Beaky, Mick and Titch.' The resident band 'The Ray Mcvay Sound' was also appearing. In the dim and distant past Ray was the MD for Larry Parnes. He worked with Gene Vincent, Eddie Cochran, Freddie Cannon, Conway Twitty and Billy Fury. Ray's drummer was often Brian Bennett (who later joined 'The Shadows.') Clem Cattini was his replacement until he too headed off for pastures new when he joined 'The Tornados.' Ray's guitarist was Colin Green who later became the MD for Shirley Bassey. On piano and vocals was Clive Powell (who later changed his name to Georgie Fame.) Ray then moved to Mecca and formed his showband. They played at many of the best-known Mecca ballrooms and then did twelve years on 'Come Dancing.' He now runs 'The Glenn Miller Orchestra' in the UK and this incarnation of the Glenn Miller sound has proved to be a busy and successful venture for Ray.

Julie Felix came to England from California in 1964 and soon signed up with Decca. A single, *Someday Soon* and an album *Julie Felix* were released and Julie started her TV appearances on 'The Eamon Andrews Show.' In '65 The Times named her 'Britain's First Lady of Folk'. She was the first British-based folk singer to fill 'The Royal Albert Hall' that same year. The next year saw her on the 'Frost Report' and in 1967 she topped the bill at 'The Saville Theatre' with Georgie Fame. Julie was the hostess of her own TV show in 1968 and was one of the acts at the Isle of Wight festival in 1969 which also saw a comeback appearance by Bob Dylan. She signed up with Mickie Most in 1970 and her single *If I Could* was the first hit from his 'RAK' label. She was busy in 1971 and '72 saw an album release where the session musicians included John Paul Jones on bass (who was later a founder member of 'Led Zeppelin' and drummer Cozy Powell (RIP)) In 1973 Julie hit the charts again with *Heaven Is Here* and guested at Hong Kong's First 'International Arts Festival.' 1974 saw her move to the 'EMI' label and she recorded an album produced by Del Newman (who was the MD for several tracks on an album called *Moonshine* by a later band of mine, 'Legend' and which was released in 1972.) Julie Felix toured extensively but in the late seventies she moved to Norway. Two successful albums were released in Sweden on the 'Scranta Gramafon' label. In the 1980's Julie moved back to California. Later she returned to her house in Hertfordshire and established the first New Age Folk Club, 'The Magic Messenger.' Julie also created the 'Remarkable Records' label and released an album called *Bright Shadows*.

'Dave Dee, Dozy, Beaky, Mick and Titch' formed in 1961 with the rather more sensible name of 'Dave Dee And The

Bostons.' The group played extensively on a semi professional basis in and around their hometown of Salisbury. Dave Dee was then a police cadet and he was one of the emergency team called to the road crash, which killed Eddie Cochran near Salisbury. The band played residencies at UK dance halls and also appeared in clubs in Germany in 1962. Their staple fare was rock and roll but they also did some comedy turns too. The supported 'The Honeycombs' on a tour in 1964 and were taken on by managers Ken Howard and Alan Blaikley. 'Fontana' records signed them up and they then had two unsuccessful singles, *No Time* and *All I Want* under their new name. At last they had a hit in the UK chart with *You Make It Move*. Twelve more hits followed. Howard & Blaikley provided songs that were moulded into different styles by DDDBM&T. Dave eventually left and the group continued without him for a while but in the 90's they came back together again. They are a very good band with tight harmonies and Dave Dee is an exceptional showman.

The Fingers also supported a chap called Guy Darrell who had a backing group known as 'The Gnomes of Zurich.' Guy had recorded a song with which he had a small hit in 1966 – *My Way of Thinking...* yes the same song that we had recorded as a B-side to *I'll Take You Where the Music's Playing*.

'Unit 4 + 2' was another band that we played with and their lovely harmonies impressed us. Unfortunately they had only one hit here, *Concrete And Clay* but it was also successful in the States too. The guitarist Brian Parker started the ball rolling with an instrumental group from Hertfordshire called 'The Hunters', who started recording on the 'Fontana' label in 1961. 'The Hunters' recorded a seminal instro called *The Storm* (1961), which used a tone and volume pedal to great effect. Parker joined Adam Faith's backing group 'The Roulettes' in

1962 but left very soon. Brian wanted to have a band with good vocals and he got together with two other guitarists, Tommy Moeller and David Meikle. They added a singer (Brian Moules) and then played locally for a time. When they went pro Brian Parker left but carried on writing with Moeller. Howard Lubin took his place in the band. In 1963 they became 'Unit Four.' Finally they decided to add two new musicians, Rod Garwood on bass and Hugh Halliday as the new drummer. 'Unit 4' no longer described the band so they added the '+2.' 1964 saw them sign up with 'Decca' and their first single *Green Fields*, was issued early that same year. This single was reasonably successful but the next one *Sorrow And Pain*, did not dent the charts at all. Then along came *Concrete And Clay*, issued early in 1965 and this was a really effective number. For this single they had two other musicians sitting in; Russ Ballard on guitar and drummer Bob Henrit. Both of these gents had been in 'The Roulettes' with Brian Parker. *Concrete And Clay* was a chart topper here and was a hit worldwide. An album was issued but there was nothing to compare with *Concrete And Clay. You've Never Been In Love Like This Before,* was their next single but it was not as successful as *Concrete And Clay*, although it did get into the UK Top 20. Other singles followed; *You've Got To Be Cruel To Be Kind*, and *Baby Never Say Goodbye*. In 1966 they released *I Was Only Playing Games* and this was a psychedelic flavoured single, which also had an orchestral accompaniment. 'Unit 4 +2' tried three more times whilst at 'Decca' for another hit but in 1966 they upped sticks and went over to 'Fontana'. More poppy singles came out and an LP. Garwood, Halliday and Meikle all left in 1967 and lo and behold who should replace them but Russ Ballard and Bob Henrit. 'Unit 4 + 2' carried on with his strong line up. In 1968 they issued a cover of the Bob Dylan song *You Ain't Going Nowhere* but they were pipped to the post in the charts by a version recorded by 'The Byrds.'. 1969 saw them release what has been described as a single "in full blown Psychedelic mode." This opus was *3.30* but it did not enter the charts. The band split up in 1969 with Ballard and Henrit resurfacing in 'Argent' (led by Rod Argent from 'The Zombies.')

Other acts were touring regularly and 'The Fingers' played with many of these at a venue in Westcliff on Sea – 'The Cliffs Pavilion.'

David Garrick was one of these acts. He had only two hits; *Dear Mrs Applebee* and *Lady Jane* (a Jagger-Richard song) both of which made Top 20 appearances in 1966. Garrick's real name was Philip Darryl Core and he came from Liverpool. He had sung in a church choir and had operatic training for four years. In 1965 he started to sing pop. He was popular with the ladies but what happened to him later I do not know. He was fairly prolific having two albums, one EP and thirteen singles between 1965 and 1969.

'Hedgehoppers Anonymous' had one hit that was produced by Jonathan King (many years before his fall from grace.) The initial line up was: Leslie Dash (drums), Ray Honeyball (bass). Alan Laud (guitar), John Stewart (lead guitar) and Mick Tilsley (vocals). Keith Jackson and Glen Martin later replaced Honeyball and Dash and then Tom Fox came in, instead of Jackson. The band had originally got together at an airbase in Bedfordshire. At first they were called 'The Trendsetters' but soon became 'The Hedgehoppers.'

In 1965, Jonathan King had written *It's Good News Week* and decided that the band should record this protest song. King added 'Anonymous' to their name group's name and Mick Tinsley and session musicians recorded the song. These session musos included none other than Jimmy Page. The record was a big hit but no others followed. 'Hedgehoppers Anonymous' issued five singles on 'Decca' but the group disbanded in 1966. (They are now playing together again.) These guys were impressed by 'The Fingers' and said that they would get Jonathan King to phone me. True to their word I had a call at home from Jonathan who said he would be interested in managing and recording the band. Jonathan King (real name Kenneth George King) was born in 1944. In 1965 he wrote & sang on his first hit, *Everyone's Gone To The Moon*. It was a huge hit worldwide. JK also discovered, produced and named 'Genesis' who were initially a band at a Public School (Charterhouse) with Peter Gabriel as lead singer. As well as having his own TV series, King then ran 'Decca' Records for some time. In 1971(and the subsequent two years) he was named Producer of the Year. He also had several hits under other names. JK also produced 'The Bay City Rollers' and sang on their first hit, *Keep On Dancing*. During the '70s he was massively successful as a well-known pop star and producer. He formed 'UK Records', and signed '10cc' to his own label. In 1975 he won the Record of the Year for his own rendition of *Una Paloma Blanca*. He ran 'Decca' again for his friend, Sir Edward Lewis, until it was sold to 'Polygram' in the late '70s. A stint in the USA and various newspaper columns added to his CV and he hosted and wrote 'The Brits' in 1987. In 1990, 1991 and 1992 he wrote & produced 'The Brits', and in 1995 he took over 'A Song For Europe.' 'A Song For Europe' led to a British Eurovision win in 1997 for 'Katrina and the Waves', *Love Shine A Light*, being the successful candidate. Many other and very varied ventures followed until in Oct 1997 he was made The Man of the Year for the British Music Industry. He has now fallen from grace and it would be inappropriate for me to add any comment to the reams of stories that have been written about his court case, which led to him being jailed. 'The Fingers' were very ethical chaps and when Jonathan phoned me I told him that we could not have him as our manager as we already had a manager – Dick Mountney. Who knows what would have happened if we had decided to ditch poor Dick and work with JK?

16.
As Psychedelic as Ken Dodd

O ur reputation as a Psychedelic band was mentioned in the music press many times but the definitive quote for me comes from the Record Mirror of 05 11 1966: 'The Fingers are about as Psychedelic as Ken Dodd.' Geoff Stephens was talked about as the songwriter of 1967 (Record Mirror – 07 01 1967) and we did some sessions for Pete recording Stephens' numbers. One was for Barry Fantoni. Barry was the person who once said "Of course I'm doing something about my overdraft: I'm seeing my accountant." He also created the hideous 'first lady of journalism', Glenda Slag, who was born in the pages of 'Private Eye.' My duties on a track called *Bench Number Three At Waterloo Station* were simply to play a roll on timpani every bar. Other sessions that we did included some for the wonderfully named 'Vernon Haddock's Jubilee Lovelies.' I sang the lead line on the choruses for an (unreleased?) recording of *You Are My Honeysuckle*. Bob Clouter and I also played with them on *I'll Be Your Baby Tonight* a Bob Dylan song, which also appeared on *Nice*. 'The Jubilee Lovelies' had one album issued in 1965 on 'Columbia' and they were a sort of spaced out jug band.

'The Merseys' (part of original 'The Merseybeats') were Tony Crane and Billy Kinsley and were another of the acts that we supported in 1967 (following a New Years' Eve ball with 'Eric Delaney's Band' at the Cliffs.) 'The Merseybeats' started in 1962 after another band called 'The Mavericks' spilt up. They soon became popular locally and were signed up by Brian Epstein. However, they did not stay with him for long as they had different ideas to those of Epstein regarding musical styles. On stage they were a meatier band than the ballads, which were associated with them, because of their records, would have had you suppose. Their first release reached 28 and *I Think Of You* was a Top Ten hit. Their later releases were perfectly respectable offerings but did not do as well as *I Think Of You*. In 1966 'The Merseybeats' disbanded, but Tony Crane and Billy Kinsley carried on as 'The Merseys'. Their biggest success was *Sorrow*, which went as high as number 4 in the spring of the same year. This was their last hit. 'The Merseybeats' later reformed with leader Tony Crane back at the helm. They still tour as a part of the regular 1960's nostalgia concerts. 'The Merseybeats' left a legacy of nine singles between 1963 and 1969, whilst 'The Merseys' had six 45's released between 66 and 69. Al of these were on the 'Fontana' label.

17.
Nigel Grog – "The Hardest Working Man In Show Business."

The Fingers' were asked to audition for a tour for one of the major pirate radio stations and the tryouts were heard in a dusty and damp church hall somewhere in the outskirts of London. The acts were many and varied and included a group called 'The Gods' with a very fine guitarist, Mick Taylor who later joined 'The Stones.' 'The God's' line up was: Brian Glascock (drums), John Glascock (bass), Ken Hensley (vocals, keyboards, guitar), Joe Konas (guitar, vocal) and Mick Taylor (guitar.) 'The Gods' issued two albums (1968 and 1969) and were formed in Hatfield in 1965. Taylor left to join 'John Mayall's Bluesbreakers' in 1967. They carried on with a new line up that included Greg Lake on bass and managed to get a residency at 'The Marquee.' However, Lake left in 1968 to join 'King Crimson.' John Glascock rejoined the band and recorded their two progressive rock albums and a few 45s.

Another group had done away with mike stands by attaching gooseneck mike holders to the horns of their guitars. They were a band from New Zealand called 'The Human Instinct.' This group was a popular hard rock/psychedelic act in their own country in the late sixties and early seventies. They originated from 'The Four Fours', who had some hits in New Zealand in the mid-1960s. They came to the UK in 1966 and became 'The Human Instinct' at the same time. 'The

Human Instinct' had three flops on 'Mercury' and then moved to 'Deram' where they unfortunately had no success either with two more singles. 'The Human Instinct' went back to NZ, reorganised their line up and headed off in a heavier direction. This version of the band also came to the UK but fared no better than the previous line up. 'The Human Instinct' kept on going and recording right into the late 1990's.

One of the bands had a pretty boy singer who the tour promoters liked but they were not happy with his band. They asked us if we would back the singer as well as appearing as 'The Fingers.' You've guessed it - we turned them down. Oh by the way the singer was - David Essex! (We were particularly good at turning down what might have been good openings.)

David has had a very varied and successful career including live concerts, records, theatre, composing, films and television. He has had twenty-three Top 30 singles in Britain alone. He appeared in the musical 'Godspell' and received two major awards for this show. David Essex acted in 'That'll Be The Day', with Ringo Starr, and the sequel 'Stardust', this time with Larry Hagman and Adam Faith. During the filming of 'That'll Be The Day', David wrote and recorded *Rock On*, which was a chart topper here and across the pond. Many other chart entries followed. One of his most well acclaimed roles was as Che in the musical 'Evita.' Over the years Essex has worked tirelessly and his tours are always sold out. In 1999 David was awarded an OBE in recognition of his services to charity, especially to VSO.

A band that had a big effect on 'The Fingers' was 'The Move', who we supported in January 1966. Their tight act featured strong harmonies and the charismatic Carl Wayne teamed with the equally wonderful Roy Wood. They played a superb doo-wop version of *Zing Went The Strings Of My Heart*, which we promptly copied and included in our stage act for some considerable time. 'The Move' had several memorable hits and a vibrant stage act. They originally teamed up in February 1966. The initial members came from other Birmingham bands and the personnel was as follows: Bev Bevan (drums), Carl Wayne (vocals), Chris "Ace" Kefford (bass), Roy Wood (lead guitar) and Trevor Burton (rhythm.) They used four or even five part harmonies (so you can see why 'The Fingers' were impressed.) The manager of 'The Moody Blues', Tony Secunda soon took 'The Move' under his wing. They came to London and started a weekly residency at 'The Marquee Club' and dressed as gangsters. 'The Move' moved away (!) from the west Coast material that they had previously favoured and headed towards a so-called psychedelic style. Secunda encouraged Roy Wood to write which was also a good move (Boom! Boom!) *Night Of Fear* the 1812 influenced song was their first single. The record zoomed to number 2. If you re-listen to 'The Move' now you will see that their records were varied, interesting and showed the incredible promise of the Roy Wood influence. 'The Move' were one of the first groups to smash things up on stage and Carl Wayne destroyed TV's with an axe in front of disbelieving crowds. *Flowers in the Rain* was the first record to be played on the new 'BBC Radio1' station (which replaced the 'BBC Light Programme.') One of their best songs, *I Can Hear The Grass Grow* was a number two hit for them. The band left Secunda and then issued *Fire Brigade*, which soared to number 3. This had Roy Wood singing lead for the first time on a single. Before the release of their first LP, Ace Kefford left the group. Trevor Burton became their new bassist and they slimmed down to a four piece. Then came the next single *Wild Tiger Woman*. This track featured session pianist Nicky Hopkins (who later played on two tracks recorded by 'The Fingers.') Unfortunately it did not make a chart appearance. The doldrums for The Move did not last long and *Blackberry Way* was a number 1 hit in November 1968. Burton was not happy with the musical direction that the band was taking and left them. Rick Price joined on bass and their next single was *Curly*, which reached no. 12. Their second album was *Shazam* with one side written by Roy Wood and the other featuring covers. *Hello Susie* and *Beautiful Daughter* were great 'Move' offerings but Carl Wayne left January 1970. I seem to recall that Carl was a milkman in the TV soap opera 'Crossroads', for a while. Thankfully he has had better roles and for example he was the narrator in the West End smash 'Phantom Of The Opera' for some time. (Unfortunately Carl is also no longer with us.) 'The Move' continued as three-piece but Jeff Lynne joined them very soon and this augured the ambitious project that he and Wood started later with 'The Electric Light Orchestra.' (Vic Collins of 'The Kursaal Flyers' had played earlier on in his career as a member of a band called 'The *Cardboard* Orchestra'!) Wood then came into prominence with the heavy song *Brontosaurus* and this was the first time that the shy guitarist used face paint. *Brontosaurus* got to number 7 in 1970. The album *Looking On* was the first to feature all own-compositions. A single When *Alice Comes Back To The Farm* featured multi-tracked cello but did not chart. Rick Price left 'The Move' as Wood and Lynne concentrated on ELO. *Message From The Country* was their final album, and they released three singles on EMI from this LP. These were *Tonight, Chinatown* and *California Man.* 'The Move' had an American hit with a song written by Jeff Lynne, *Do Ya* but over here it was the B-side of *California Man. California Man* did get to no. 7 just as the debut single by 'ELO', *10538 Overture*, charted. Roy Wood still plays live (but not very frequently) in a large band with seven or so young girls in mini-skirts. But fear not! They all come from 'The National Jazz Youth Orchestra' and are great musicians as well as being very decorative. Carl Wayne sang with 'The Hollies' for a while until his untimely death.

Another memorable night for The Fingers' was a Big L party night at Billy Walker's club 'The Upper Cut' in Forest Gate in a cold and dank February 1966, where we supported 'The Symbols'. 'The Symbols' were a good harmony band who were originally named 'Johnny Milton and The Condors. They released one album and nine singles. Their first two singles were on 'Columbia' but all the other releases came out on the 'President' label. They issued their offerings between 1965 and 1968. This Essex group had a minor hit with a cover of 'The Ronettes' song *Best Part Of Breaking Up*. 'The Symbols' also had another minor hit which was a cover of 'The Four Seasons' *Bye Bye Baby*. Their personnel included Joe Baccini (bass), Mick Clarke (bass – who later became a 'Rubette'), Sean Corrigan (guitar), Clive Graham (drums), Johnny Milton (vocals), Rikki Smith (guitar) and Chas. Wade Drums.)

The bill at 'The Upper Cut' was varied and also included a 'Ready Steady Go' connection as 'Patrick Kerr's Go-Go Girl Dancers' were appearing. It was a fashion at the time to have scantily clad girlies shimmying to the latest records especially when the venue could not afford to employ a proper band. Patrick Kerr used to demonstrate new dances like 'The Hitch Hiker' on 'Ready Steady Go' and he also appeared on package tours like the Sandie Shaw/Adam Faith one in 1965, which also included 'The Barron Knights', 'The Paramounts', (who backed Sandie Shaw for a time) and 'The Roulettes' (who were Adam Faith's backing band at the time.). Nowadays of course scantily clad is stark naked if need be and a lot of fashionable clubs use DJ's as a matter of choice. How times have changed!

Another club that we played at was 'Tiles' in Oxford Street (a club where 'Pink Floyd', 'The Who and Simon Dupree also played at around the same time.)

'The Creation' was another band that appeared at the 'Cliffs'. I understand that their lead guitarist used to play his guitar with a violin bow but I can't honestly say whether or not he did so that night. (Jimmy Page later also used Eddie Phillips' trick of using a violin bow.) Eddie Phillips was the guitarist of 'The Creation', who evolved from a group known as 'Mark Four.' The group changed their name to 'The Creation' in 1966 when they made a record deal with 'Planet Records'. 'Planet Records' was Shel Talmy's label and Shel was already known as the producer of 'The Kinks' and 'The Who'. 'The Creation' also had one of their members, Kenny Pickett painting canvasses with aerosol paint on stage and he would then set them on fire. Ronnie Wood (later in 'The Rolling Stones') joined them in 1968.

'The Tremeloes' were (and still are) a good band with a very proficient lead guitarist in Rick West. We supported them at least twice; once in Westcliff on Sea and again in Frankfurt (more of that later.) By then they had parted company with Brian Poole but were becoming experts at the harmonies that they used most elegantly on *Silence Is Golden*. 'Brian Poole And The Tremeloes' were already a chart-topping group and when he left in 1966 things could have gone pear-shaped for the Trems. However, they blazed a new position for themselves with a line-up of: Rick West (guitar), Alan Blakely (rhythm guitar), Dave Munden (drums) and Alan Howard (bass.) In May of 1966 Mike Clark replaced Howard, but three months later Clark was replaced by Len 'Chip' Hawkes. Their debut single as 'The Tremeloes' (without BP) was *Blessed*. This single obviously wasn't, as it was not a hit. They then recorded 'The

Beatles' song *Good Day Sunshine.* This did not chart either. The third Trems only release, *Here Comes My Baby* (written by Cat Stevens) entered the Top 10 here and in the USA. A brave follow up was *Silence Is Golden.* This had been the flip-side to a single by 'The Four seasons', *Rag Doll.* It is not an easy number to do well and uses falsetto harmonies that are difficult to pitch and to project but they made an excellent job of the song, so much so that they had their only number one with this single. A good run of hits followed during the late 60s including *Even The Bad Times Are Good, Suddenly You Love Me, Helule Helule* and *My Little Lady.* They then began to write their own material and *(Call Me) Number One,* went to number two. 'The Tremeloes' had a mild flirtation with heavy, progressive music and the LP *Master* is an example of that phase. *Me And My Life* was a final Top Twenty effort. They still tour as part of the 60's nostalgia circuit. Groucho Marx famously said, "Nostalgia isn't what it used to be." In this case it is, as they are a very good band.

On one of 'The Fingers' gigs somewhere in the Home Counties we played alongside a band called 'The Maze' who featured some very polished songs in the 'Tamla Motown' vein. They had musicians in the band that later became part of the first version of 'Deep Purple' – Rod Evans and Ian Paice.

'The Maze' had previously been known as 'MI5' and used to play at the '2B's' Club in Ashford (which may have been where we first came across them as 'The Fingers' used to play there too.) Their line up was as follows: Chris Banham (keyboards), Rod Evans (vocals), Eric 'Jack' Keene (bass), Roger Lewis (guitar) and Ian Paice (drums.) 'The Maze' played together from 1966 to 1968 and released three singles here plus an EP that was recorded in Italy but issued in France. I recall that one of their singles was a well-crafted version of the Barbara Lewis song, *Hello Stranger.*

'Pinkerton's (Assorted) Colours' came and went at the Cliffs and as usual we played as the middle act of the night. The general drill at this venue was that there would be a chart name (or a well known band on the way up or down!) 'The Fingers' would play in the middle spot as a reasonably popular local attraction and there would also be another band such as 'The Spooks' or 'Sounds Around.' The line up for 'Pinkerton's Assorted Colours' was: Samuel "Pinkerton" Kempe (autoharp/vocals), Tony Newman (guitar), Tom Long (guitar), Barrie Bernard (bass guitar) and John Wallbank/Dave Holland (drums.) 'Pinkerton's Colours' (as they became known later) also used an Autoharp, just like 'The Fingers.' Mr. Kempe had started to use this instrument after it had been introduced into pop by 'The Lovin' Spoonful.' It was probable that Pete Eden's suggestion that 'The Fingers' should use the Autoharp also came from the same influence. As 'The Liberators', they formed up in 1964 in Rugby. One single was issued under this name. Their manager Reg Calvert, who also managed 'The Fortunes', changed their name. (I prefer the original name and so I suspect did they!) In late 1965 they signed up with Decca and released *Mirror, Mirror,* which reached no. 9 in the charts in December 1965. Their follow up, *Don't Stop Loving Me Baby* (1966) was a more marginal success (at no. 50) but the last single, (also 1966) *Magic Rocking Horse* failed to chart. They dropped the 'Assorted' tag and moved to 'Pye' but had no further hits.

'Sounds Around' eventually became 'Peter and The Wolves.' They recorded two singles under the name 'Sounds Around' and these were *What Does She Do?* (1966) and *Red White And You* (1967). Both of these missives came out on the 'Piccadilly' label. Their bass player was Nick Ryan and he was the man who sang, "Give 'em a lift mmmm with Cookeen." He also came up with the idea for *Just One Cornetto.* Nick now lives in Ireland. Another talented member was John Pantry. John released two albums and four singles in the first half of the seventies on the 'Philips' label. He has also been involved in producing and playing on various religious albums over the years some of which feature Mo Witham. As 'Peter and The Wolves' they released five singles on the 'MGM' label. They later became known as 'Factory' and also recorded as 'Norman Conquest.' Their last single came out as 'Wolfe.'

'The Fingers' also played on the same bill as 'Neil Christian and the Crusaders', whose most famous guitarist (a 'Knees Club' member!) was Jimmy Page (pre-'Led Zeppelin'.) Neil Christian's real name was the rather more prosaic Christopher Tidmarsh and he was born in 1943. Their original guitarist was Jimmy Page, as mentioned above and he played on Neil's 1964 release, *Honey Hush* as a session man. Albert Lee, Mick Abrahams and Alex Dmochowski (later of 'Aynsley Dunbar Retaliation',) all played in 'The Crusaders' along the way. Ritchie Blackmore (guitar), Elmer Twitch (piano), Bibi Blange (bass) and Tornado Evans (drums) backed him on his live dates to promote his hit tune *That's Nice. That's Nice* got to number UK Top 20 in 1966, but Neil's follow up *Oops* did not chart. Christian moved to Germany and there he was extremely successful. When he did return to the UK Neil Christian continued to record but with little success and he then stopped performing.

We also supported 'The Nashville Teens', again at our own stomping ground 'The Cliffs Pavilion'. They were formed in 1962, in Weybridge. They had two lead singers (Ray Phillips and Arthur Sharp.) In 1966 drummer Barry Jenkins left to join 'The Animals', and pianist John Hawken formed 'Renaissance' with Keith Relf (formerly of 'The Yardbirds'.) Art Sharp left in the early 1970's to become a record producer and Ray Phillips is the only original 'Teen' member. Their first record was as a backing band for Jerry Lee Lewis (following their initiation into the Hamburg scene at 'The Star Club'.) They also recorded with Carl Perkins. Their most famous record is without a doubt the song, *Tobacco Road* that they rearranged and it became one of the best-known R&B standards. 'The Nashville Teens' produced many records during the sixties and seventies and worked with top notch producers and managers like Mickie Most, Don Arden, Andrew Loog Oldham, and Shel Talmy. The band also toured in the States with stars like Bo Diddley, Ben E King and Chuck Berry.

The Fingers were working through the 'Arthur Howes Agency' at this time and they had acts like the following names on their books:

- 'The Walker Brothers'
- 'The Kinks'
- 'Dave Dee, Dozy, Beaky, Mick and Titch'
- Helen Shapiro
- Simon Dupree
- Guy Darrell
- 'The Flies'
- 'Ebony Keyes'
- 'Winston's Fumbs'

At about this time 'The Fingers' were inveigled into doing some publicity shots in Hyde Park resplendent in our normal hats and braces and wielding a variety of instruments including a double bass that I never could play anyway.

The Fingers in Hyde Park – 1967
Back – Mo Witham, Centre Row – Alan Beecham, Bob
Clouter, John Bobin, Next: Dave Grout, Front Rick Mills

Ricky and Dave decided to move down to Southend as

the travelling from South Ockenden (their home town) was becoming a nuisance and they found a small upstairs flat in Westcliff on Sea (just outside Southend.) The landlord, coincidentally, was Bert Ballard, who had been engaged to my Mum when she was very young. Ricky and Dave's flat only had one bedroom but it did see some coming and going. All of this activity was primarily fuelled by chip butties and coffee as neither Dave nor Ricky were very good cooks. The flat under Ricky and Dave's was occupied by a poor old soul called Mrs. Fisher. She had the knack of putting bright red lipstick almost anywhere other than her lips and was basically bonkers. She was convinced that the lads were going to kill her and even called the police one day. Ricky didn't help by telling her that the guitar cases had guns inside. We invited her for a drink one Christmas but she thought she would be poisoned and refused to come upstairs. Dave was becoming bored with his guitar and hit upon an ideal way to change it without having to buy a new one. Every now and then he would take off all the hardware and then respray it a new colour using car paint. This looked great - from a distance. Another one of my old pals, Bob Heath from 'The Rhet Stoller Group' went even further. He drilled huge circular holes through his 'Fender Stratocaster.' I can't imagine that this helped with its resale value and it might have affected the sustain of the notes which (allegedly at least) is improved by having certain kinds of woods for the guitar body but not by having bloody great holes. Eventually Dave wanted a real change and bought a 'Gibson Stereomaster' from Joe Macari's shop in Denmark Street. Denmark Street is 'the' street as far as musical associations go. In the 1920's it started to be called 'Tin Pan Alley' but it was originally known as the main place to go to for sheet music. Music publishers moved there around the turn of the century but in the 1930s, shops also started to sell musical instruments. Recording studios gravitated there in the 1960s. 'The Rolling Stones' recorded their first LP at 'Regent Sounds' Studio. The street still has musical connotations with recording studios, publishers and manufacturers still being present.

Mo began to experiment with lighter strings by using a 'Clifford Essex' banjo string instead of his top E string and 'destringing.' This was a fairly common trick before the manufacturers started to make different gauge strings and it involved using an E for a B and a B for a G string. This made it easier to bend the notes and to play in the bluesy style that was becoming more and more prevalent. It also caused huge tuning difficulties as the strings used to go flat very easily. Keeping strings live and bright was always a problem for young bands that could not afford to replace them as often as they would like. The solution adopted by many guitarists (especially bass players) was to take off the old strings and to boil them. Once they were replaced they were then brighter – oh for at least a couple of days. Duck Dunn of 'Booker T and the MG's' was once asked how often he replaced his strings and he said he changes them "about every fifteen years." Bass players all have different opinions. Some people change strings very frequently whilst others only change them when they break. Other famous bassists that did not like replacing their strings were James Jamerson and Herbie Flowers. James Jamerson told his son (also a bass player), "Never change your strings or clean your bass. You don't want to take any of that funk off it." Herbie Flowers used to use the black nylon wound strings and said that he used them for so long that the wrappings would wear away. Bassists in those days used flat (or tape) wound strings that had a smooth but sometimes lifeless sound. Another variation was a type of string that was wound with a black nylon covering. When round wound bass strings were invented in 1962 most bassists changed over to them and are still using them today. You can buy bass strings today in various different gauges but the light gauge strings are only really suitable for plinky plonky show offs and don't have a very full sound.

In Ricky and Dave's flat there was a piano, which nobody except for Alan could play. When we were drunk late at night we would raise a hell of a din by creating 'music for horror films' with this piano. Ricky just could not get up in the mornings and he rigged up a complicated affair that caused an alarm clock to rattle a tray, that would cause something else to fall off and it would then switch on a radio that was connected to a high volume amp. I am not certain that this ever worked but it was ingenious. Ricky was a great one for the ladies. He had big brown eyes and a soulful expression and they couldn't resist him. One day he and Dave picked up a couple of girls and we found out that they were living on an ex-gunboat with some lads, moored on a creek near Leigh on Sea. One of these girls was a very sweet natured and kind person called Noreen (or Norrie for short) and I think the other was called Barbara and she was an altogether much more formidable woman. One thing led to another and they moved into Rick and Dave's flat. Although Barbara stayed for a relatively short period of time, Norrie was a long-term fixture for Ricky and she eventually became pregnant. Ricky and Norrie used to call the unborn baby 'Nairn' as she said it felt like a bubble inside her and there was a floor covering at the time made by Nairn that had bubbles in the manufacturing process somewhere, to make the flooring feel soft. After a while they invented a new name for the baby, 'Blodwyn.' Now in those days having a baby out of wedlock was still frowned upon and Norrie was booked into a nursing home out of Southend so that she could have the baby and then the plan was for the baby to be quietly put up for adoption. Whilst Norrie was at the nursing home, we played at a club called 'The Witchdoctor', in Catford. In the audience there was a striking blond girl with very long hair called Rita (the girl not the hair!) She was wearing what was probably a grey faux fur coat but she did look good and Ricky took her home where he rose to the challenge.

PA speakers in the mid sixties for gigging bands that carried their own gear were usually fairly modest. They were usually two, line-source 'Vox', 'Selmer' or 'Watkins' made cabinets and the amps were also very low wattage affairs of 100 watts or so. 'Vox' was one of the greatest amp manufacturers in the 1960's and their amps were used by such acts as 'The Rolling Stones', 'The Beatles' and 'The Shadows'. The 'Vox' story started in 1941 but it is the 'Vox AC30' that is the most famous of all their amps. It was in late 1959 that 'The Shadows' acquired three 'AC30's.' 'Celestion' had developed a new speaker using an alnico magnet and painted blue. This was pivotal to the 'Vox sound and its success. When "Apache" reached number 1 in 1960 'Vox' amps became known as *the* best British amplifiers.

'Watkins' amps were also used by many famous acts such as 'The Who' and 'Fleetwood Mac.' 'Watkins' amps were marketed as 'WEM' (Watkins Electric Music.) The way ahead for huge PA set-ups was virtually invented by Charlie Watkins but his early combos such as the 'Dominator' and the 'Joker' were very popular with gigging bands. 'WEM' started in the early 50's. With the advent of skiffle, 'WEM' really took off. Many guitarists who wanted a different sound used their 'Copicat' Echo Unit. They also produced valve amps like the 17-Watt 'Dominator.' For a while the 'Watkins Rapier' guitar was the only viable alternative to the 'Hofner Futurama' for guitarists who could not afford a Strat. Charlie Watkins used the technique known as "slaving" of amps to create high-powered P.A. Systems in 1964, which is a principle that is still used today.

Ricky decided to make some new cabinets and we ended up with 4, 2 X 12 cabinets which were stuffed with glass fibre wool which made your hands itch like mad if you touched it without wearing gloves.

Dick Mountney also introduced us to a tall dignified looking cove with a beard called George Bird. George became a very good singer and I played with him for quite a time in a band called 'Amber' years later. At this time however, he was singing with a voice that he had adopted in a strangled P J Proby mode and it was not nearly as god as his normal voice. Dick wanted us to record a demo for George so we trooped up to the rehearsal room at 'The Cricketers' and laid down a simple version of a song called *I'm Just A Drifter*. This was done using Dick's reel-to-reel 'Revox' tape recorder. I wonder if that recording still exists?

18.

Three Irish Beauties And Other Adventures

At about this time we came to know three lovely Irish sisters, Julie, Ann and Maureen Kearney who lived on Canvey Island when they started to come to 'The Elms' to see us. I went out with Julie. Bob and Ann were together for some time and I seem to recall a lad called Martin being very friendly with Maureen. Martin had one hand, following a tragic accident when he was younger and which happened when he was cleaning some machinery at work, which was switched on whilst his hand was inside the machine. Martin made the most of his life and drove a car with an attachment like a ball that fitted into a socket fixed to the steering wheel. He and I were very friendly at the time and he frequently gave me a lift home to my parents' house where we would sit in the kitchen drinking coffee until the small hours. Julie was an absolute cracker. She was very dark and just like the actress Samantha Eggar. I was in love again! Ever since my hormonal sap started to rise as a young teenager I have found it very easy to fall in love and much harder to get over a broken relationship. I am also a serial settler down, which has resulted in three marriages. (My wife now, Pauline as I have said before is the last and best without a doubt.) Julie and I canoodled all over the place but I never got the first prize so when I was teased in the van about my non-existent sexual exploits I used to change the subject.' Look at that nice tree!' I would say. Julie and I lasted a few months and it was my jealousy that caused us to split. I knew she was going to go to a party when I was playing elsewhere and I asked a friend, Frank, to make sure she didn't get up to mischief. Frank told her that I was concerned and she felt that I was being unreasonable so she promptly dumped me.

At about this time *I Go To Sleep* was released in Italy (and elsewhere on the continent for all I know) and sank without a trace.

One night at the 'Cliffs' a blonde girl called Helga pinched one of my shoes. She did this whilst we were playing and told me that I would have to chase her for it. These lovely shoes were green and orange phosphorescent beasts that were in fact old 'Hush Puppies' that I had painted myself. I seem to remember that in order to get the shoe back I had to take Helga to the group's van parked near the stage door. We were soon puffing and panting in the van when Helga promptly said that she felt very sorry for me as musicians had so many sexual conquests that there was no real feeling in the actual event for them. She said that this union had to be special and taken at a more measured and thoughtful pace so she thought we ought not to consummate our very new relationship just yet. If only she knew that I was actually a very inexperienced youngster and although I had enjoyed many episodes of what used to be called 'heavy petting' I was a virgin! We left the van and obviously got some stick from the other members of the group but I don't think I ever saw her again.

'Timebox' was another excellent band that played at 'The Cliffs Pavilion. They released various singles but their five UK releases were later issued as an album called, *One Original Moose on The Loose*. 'Timebox' were: Clive Griffiths (bass), Pete "Ollie" Halsall, (guitar), John Halsey (drums), Chris Holmes (piano) and Mike Patto (vocals.) They issued seven singles between

1966 and 1969. 'Piccadilly' released the first two and the others were on 'Deram.' One of these ditties was the splendidly named *Baked Jam Roll In Your Eye.* They were formed in 1966 and their most well known record was a cover of a Four Seasons song, *Beggin'* In 1969 Chris Holmes left and they became Patto.

I was interviewed for an article about Psychedelia in 'Melody Maker', which surfaced in October 1966. I had been forewarned by Pete Eden that the interviewer, Chris Welch, was a jazz enthusiast and that provided I managed to say something about Charlie Mingus he would probably use my words of wisdom. Came the day, I waffled on about distortion, fuzz boxes and Charlie Mingus and my piece was used alongside an interview with the much more famous Graham Nash (of 'The Hollies.')

'The Fingers' used to enjoy playing the odd comedy numbers. At one time we did a small set by 'The hardest working man in show business – Nigel Grog.' Nigel was Ricky in a dirty old mac with a flat cap and the most hideous expression that Ricky could muster. Dave and I played ukeles and we gave immaculate renditions of George Formby songs like *When I'm Cleaning Windows.* In the same tradition we played *They're Coming To Take Me Away!* This tasteless, but very funny, monologue was a hit for Napoleon XIV but we made it our own by me wearing an old teacher's black gown and screeching the chorus lines at the top of my manic voice. This gown had been kindly given to me by my old English master Mr. Sheldrake (whose nickname was the obvious 'Bombduck.' I don't think he was related to the first guitarist of 'The Orioles', Dougie Sheldrake.) Sometimes I would throw twigs at the audience and one night I overdid this and hit a huge rugby player with a branch of a tree that we had just pulled off outside the dance hall at 'The Elms.' He came looking for me at the end of the gig as I quaked behind a 'Selmer Goliath' bass cabinet. (These speaker cabinets were originally covered in a crocodile finish but later versions were black and sliver. The first versions had an 18" speaker but later models also had a 12" speaker installed to improve the top end response.) Ricky told him I had gone home. 'Goliaths' were huge considering the originals could only handle 50 watts and as they contained just one 18" speaker the sound was deep and booming and could get rather woolly. I used two of these beasts at the time and stacked them sideways on, so the floor would really rumble but the sound was much more indistinct than the sound adopted much later by bassists who wanted to prove how clever they were by playing thousands of notes a minute.

When we started playing it was all about the feel of the music and the joy of communication. All musicians know that when they are going down well there is something in the air that makes them play better which in turn encourages the audience to dance and to enjoy the music even more. Conversely if the night is going badly there is a downward spiral and if we had such a night then there was always a bitter post mortem that even had us telling each other off for making mistakes in such and such a bar or at the beginning of a middle eight. This was very negative and forgot that once a note is played in a live environment it is gone and never to be heard again.

Mo used to refer to the musicians who were trying to be clever as playing "butterfly music' i.e. thousands of notes that mean absolutely nothing. The classic example of a guitarist who plays with economy and where every note counts is B B King. One note from him and you know who is playing. The other good example at the time was 'Booker T and the MG's'. Mick Jupp always said that they sounded as if they were playing in deck chairs and wondering if they could be bothered to play the next note!

This Could Be A Big Drag was another comedy song, written by Pete Eden that we played and I always wore a pith helmet for this tune. Pete had also been involved in the writing of another glorious anthem called *Who Can Beat The Heap?* This tune borrowed the famous circus opening theme and went something like this:

Heap is big and Heap is woolly
Heap is a great big nasty bully
Who can fight him?
Who can smite him?
Who can beat the Heap?

'Manfred Mann' was a band that was very popular back then and one night in Ramsgate we supported the band who were appearing at 'The Supreme Ballroom.' Their first line up as Manfred Mann was; Mike Hugg (drums), Paul Jones (vocals/harmonica), Manfred Mann (keyboards) Dave Richmond (bass) and Mike Vickers (guitar.)

Formed at the tail end of 1962, this band was originally called 'The Mann- Hugg Blues Menn.' 'The Mann-Hugg Blues Menn' became popular on the growing R& B circuit and in early 1963 they signed up with HMV and changed their name to 'Manfred Mann.' (Manfred Mann was also the stage name of their South African keyboard player (real name Manfred Lubowitz.)) They had no joy with their first two singles but they hit the no. 5 slot with their next effort, *54321* which was written as the theme tune for 'Ready Steady Go!' Their bass player Dave Richmond left after *54321* and Tom McGuiness replaced him on their next single, *Hubble Bubble Toil And Trouble*. This track just missed the Top 10. *Do Wah*

Diddy Diddy is probably their most well remembered single and it topped the charts both here and in the States. After *Do Wah Diddy Diddy* came *Sha La La* and this made number 3 in the UK and number 12 across the pond. The first offering from the band in 1965 was *Come Tomorrow.* This was also a successful release as it made number 5 in the UK. Their next hit (also in 1965) was, *Oh No Not My Baby* a cover of a very good song first recorded by Maxine Brown. The last single that they released in 1965 was a Bob Dylan song, *If You Gotta Go, Go Now. My Little Red Book* was issued in August 1965 but it was not a hit. In late 1965 Mike Vickers left 'Manfred Mann', Tom McGuiness moved to guitar and Jack Bruce joined on bass. *Pretty Flamingo* was the next 45 and hit the top of charts in the UK. It was also reasonably successful in the USA. Despite this continued success Paul Jones left to go solo at the end of July 1966. Jack Bruce also left to become one of the founder members of 'Cream'. Mike D'Abo, from 'A Band Of Angels' came in as the new lead singer and Klaus Voormann (formerly with 'Paddy, Klaus and Gibson') was the new bass player. The band also left 'HMV' and moved to 'Fontana.' ('HMV' retaliated by putting out a 45 that actually included two unfinished songs.) Mike D'Abo has a very distinctive voice and his presence helped them to get over the loss of a popular singer in Paul Jones. The first single for their new label was *Just Like A Woman* (another Bob Dylan song.) This entered the Top 10 and they followed that release with *Semi-detached Suburban Mr. James* (which was written by Geoff Stephens) and which got to number 2 in the UK charts. *Ha Ha Said The Clown* was 'Manfred Mann's' first single of 1967 and it became a number 5 hit. The next two singles did not do as well but *The Mighty Quinn* (yet another Dylan sing) topped the UK charts and got to number 10 in the USA. *My Name Is Jack* was the next hit and it was a Top Ten success. In early 1969 the band were back in the charts again at number 5 with *Fox On The Run.* Their last hit single was *Ragamuffin Man* and reached number 8 here. Mann and Hugg left to form 'Manfred Mann Chapter Three' and Tom McGuiness departed to form 'McGuiness Flint.' Mike D'Abo went off to pursue a solo career. Klaus Voormann joined 'The Plastic Ono Band. ' 'Manfred Mann' was a very prolific band. They also released eight LP's and ten EP's between 1963 and 1971. Various band members now tour as 'The Manfreds' with both lead singers, Paul Jones and Mike D'Abo.

Now I'm sure Paul is a nice guy but he does have this cock-sure arrogance on stage that can get right up people's noses. We were told by one of his band at the Ramsgate gig that at a booking a few days before a punter had unplugged the leads from the PA speaker cabinets so he didn't have to listen to Paul singing. Jack Bruce (the ace bass player) was at that time a fairly uncomfortable temporary member of 'Manfred Mann' but he told us that he was currently in the process of forming a new band with a very well known blues guitarist. He said that he could not let us know who it was but that we should look in the musical press very soon. The band that he was forming was soon announced as Cream; with the blues 'God' – the great Eric 'Slowhand' Clapton. Jack also had a band later with Robin Trower who had thrilled us all as the lead guitarist of 'The Paramounts' in the sixties. Robin was a great Jimi Hendrix (RIP) fan but to my mind he became a better guitarist than Jimi.

'The Koobas' also came and went at the famous 'Cliffs.' They emanated from Liverpool and were originally called 'The Kubas'. Part of the group had been in a Liverpool group called 'The Thunderbeats', which coincidentally was one of the names that was used by 'The Phantoms' when we wanted to rename our first band. Roy Morris and Stuart Leathwood both played guitar and sang, Tony Riley was the drummer and Keith Ellis was the bassist for 'The Koobas.' 'The Koobas' released seven singles under this name between 1965 and 1968. The first three were on 'Pye' and the remainder were issued by 'Columbia.' They also issued an LP in 1969 after the band had spilt up! Keith Ellis was later in 'Van Der Graaf Generator' for a brief period. 'The Koobas' played at 'The Star Club' in Hamburg in 1963 and were signed to Brian Epstein. They also appeared in the 'Gerry & The Pacemakers' film 'Ferry Cross The Mersey.' In 1965 they supported 'The Beatles' on their final British tour. 'The Koobas' disbanded in 1968.

'The Fingers' appeared at a Christmas Eve Ball for 1967 with Kenny Baxter's band. Kenny Baxter was (and is) a well-known jazz saxophonist who has been happily married to Antoinette (yes MY Antoinette) for about four hundred years.

At this time 'The Fingers' were part of the roster for the 'Arthur Howes Agency.' This well known agency had played a big part in the 'package' tours where various, sometimes quite incongruous acts were sent out on tour together to cinemas and theatres throughout the UK such as 'The Odeon' in Southend. I saw 'The Beatles' there (twice) and also (on different occasions) Ella Fitzgerald, Ray Charles, Bo Diddley and Chuck Berry. The cinemas of those days were ideal for touring shows, as they were often very large venues.

19.
Mickie Most Loses Out!

Now comes what is probably our biggest missed opportunity. After playing at a Carnival Dance in Stoke by Nayland we were told that the agent for 'The Animals' was going to pass our details to Mickie Most. Mickie already had a successful stable of acts including 'Herman's Hermits', Lulu and 'The Animals' so we thought it most unlikely that he would be interested in us. Mickie Most was a huge influence on many acts. It was he who discovered 'The Animals' and 'The Nashville Teens' and he produced many acts such as Donovan, Lulu and Jeff Beck. Mickie's real name was Michael Hayes and he was born in Aldershot. As a teenager he formed 'The Most Brothers' with Alex Murray. In1959 he married a South African woman and emigrated. While in South Africa he was in a rock group, which played covers of American hits. He did not become an international star but he did have 11 consecutive number ones on the South African charts. Most came back to the UK in 1962 and found 'The Animals' in a Newcastle club. They recorded *Baby, Let Me Take You Home* and *House of the Rising Sun*, and the latter was a huge success. Mickie then produced *I'm Into Something Good* for Herman's Hermits and *Tobacco Road* for the Nashville Teens and, in 1966, he produced Donovan's LP *Sunshine Superman* album. (By then Donovan had parted company with Peter Eden.) Mickie Most also produced Jeff Beck in the late '60's. At the tail end of the decade he then formed 'RAK' records. The 'RAK' label was adept at releasing hits and the main writers Nicky Chinn and Mike Chapman churned out popular songs for acts like Suzi Quatro and 'Mud'. (Mo Witham from 'The Orioles' and 'The Fingers' played with Suzi for some time later on.) 'Hot Chocolate' was a successful band in the 70's for Mickie Most and they had two Top Ten entries. Mickie sold 'RAK' and then spent time on the management of the publishing rights that he had acquired over the years. On June 30, 2003, Mickey Most died of cancer, at 64. You can imagine that we did not really believe that a man as successful as Mickie Most would be interested in 'The Fingers.' However, one night we were playing at a dumpy dancehall at the back of a pub in the Edgware Road, when who should stroll in but Mickie Most. He leaned nonchalantly on a pillar stage left and left after a few numbers without making contact with any of the band. We thought he was not interested until I had a phone call from him at home. He liked the band and wanted to send us to Germany for a while to tighten us up. The way he worked, he said, was that he wanted to be our manager, agent, record producer and publisher. He said that in return he would make us stars. But I again took the ethical (= naïve) position that we already had a local manager in Dick Mountney that we couldn't just dump. Another golden opportunity vanished into haze...

20.
"Beat, Beat, Beat"

Beat, Beat, Beat' was an American Forces Network TV show that was broadcasted from Frankfurt. We were booked to play on an eclectic bill that included Don Storer and Cherry Wainer, Sue and Sunny, 'The Tremeloes' and

'The Equals.' I still have a telegram that was sent to us by my Mum and Dad wishing us all the best. Deustche Bundepost had some trouble spelling basic words and the message reads: "Good Lick Goys = Mim Dad Kids and Mary."

Don Storer and Cherry Wainer played drums and organ respectively for 'Lord Rockingham's XI' who were the house band for the early TV Rock and Roll show 'Oh Boy.' ' Lord Rockingham's X1' had a number one hit with the instrumental *Hoots Mon*. This had the immortal and politically incorrect words spoken in the middle of the tune: *Hoots Mon, there's a moose loose aboot this hoose!*

Sue and Sunny were attractive girl singers who made their own records and who also supplied oohs and ahs (as backing singers) for artists like Dusty Springfield, Tom Jones, Lulu, 'Love Affair', 'Mott the Hoople' and Elton John. Dark and vivacious, they should never have been hidden behind the myriad of other artists that they backed and they deserved whatever success they achieved in their own rights later. Their moment of glory when they were doing these vocal backing sessions was for Joe Cocker. His smash hit *With a Little Help From My Friends* had a little help from Sue and Sunny. It also featured Barrie Wilson from 'The Paramounts' on drums and Matthew Fisher on 'Hammond' organ (with whom Barrie (as B J Wilson) played in 'Procol Harum.') Sue and Sunny (who were real sisters) were also later key members of 'Brotherhood of Man.'

'The Equals' came from East London and were an R&B flavoured pop group that had elements of ska and bluebeat. At the time that we played with them in Germany they had no bass player. The lead vocalist Eddy Grant was their strong point and he did well even after he left them. Eddie was born in British Guyana and came to England when he was 12. At 16 he formed 'The Equals' with Lincoln Gordon (guitar), his twin brother Dervin Gordon (originally the vocalist), Pat Lloyd (guitar, then bass), and drummer John Hall. From 1965, 'The Equals' began playing in Europe and their first single on 'President Records' was *Hold Me Closer.* This little ditty was not a hit but DJ's flipped it over and later (1967) *Baby, Come Back* became a chart topper in Germany and Holland. In 1968 *Baby Come Back* also became a number one in Britain and slightly bruised the US charts. Later singles were not as catchy as BCB but they did have two more Top Ten hits: *Viva Bobby Joe* and *Black Skin Blue Eyed Boys.* Eddie Grant left 'The Equals' in 1971, and they continued although they had no more hits. There were some personnel changes and drummer Ronald Telemacque and guitarists Dave Martin and Frankie Hepburn were in the band later on.

The 'Beat Beat Beat' producers in Frankfurt asked us to play *I'll Take You Where the Music's Playing* and *All Kinds of People* but we pleaded with them to let us do something more representative of our stage act. Eventually they relented and we did *Most Likely You Go Your Way and I Go Mine*, a Bob Dylan song and *What Is The Reason?* from 'The Young Rascals.' Both these songs have turned up on compilation albums. One of them was *The Early Days of Rock Vol I*" (Living Legend Records) and although I know that Volume 2 was issued in 1989, I am not certain of the release date of Volume 1, which featured 'The Fingers.' These tracks also appeared on a French CD *Nowhere Men Vol 4 – British Beat 1964 -1968* which was released in 2001. We didn't even know that they were being recorded! After the gig 'The Fingers' and 'The Tremeloes' went boozing at a local club but I stayed at the local digs when the others went out to party so I could write to my sweetheart of the moment. (Mug!) This lady was a sexy young filly called Dot. Our roadie at the time, Fred, took great delight in calling us Spot and Dot as I was suffering from teenage acne at the time. Dot was my first real love and we spent many a happy Wednesday morning at her parents' flat in Chelmsford when she had a morning off. She had also a frightening friend called Senga who was like a very fierce Wanda Ventham. I found out later that Senga's real name was Agnes, which doesn't sound quite so exotic the right way round. Dot and I stayed together for about two years and we became engaged at about the time that I left 'The Fingers.' I was convinced that I was going to give up playing live and tinkered with classical guitar for a short while. By the way I was never a very good classical guitarist so John Williams didn't have to worry after all. Dot decided to call a halt to our love affair and although we did see each other once or twice a week after that, our hearts were not really in the relationship. One night we finally decided to part company and just as we did so the music over the pub's PA changed to *Love Is A Many Splendoured Thing*. I have never seen her since then except once shortly after we split up for good when I saw her in Southend

High Street. My heart went boom – as they say. I was really affected by seeing her again but we did not speak apart from to say Hi!

Ricky decided to form a group to play a sophisticated song list including numbers by Sergio Mendes, Harry Belafonte and other more cabaret-influenced artists. This was a band known rather incongruously for a guitar-based band as 'The Original String Quartet.' He asked Bob Clouter and me to join but we decided to form a covers band, 'Match' with some friends including Mark Mills (of The Phantoms') and Dougie Sheldrake (from the original 'Orioles' line up.) Dougie played a virginal in 'Match' and we had a fine jazz guitarist, Mickey Peters to fill the axe spot. (Mickey also had a very pretty sister who later on sang with 'Match' but this was after I had left to join 'Legend.')

At about this time Mick (now rebadged Mickey) Jupp recorded an acoustic album on 'Bell' records that was originally going to be issued under the name of *The Living Legend Of M G Jupp*. This first 'Legend' album featured his old pal Chris East on acoustic guitar and this reminds me of an incident that caused a little excitement when Chris was staying with Mickey in a house that was rented from Dennis Knott during the first version of 'The Orioles.' Chris was in the Navy and had gone AWOL and when some friendly naval heavies came to collect him he had to run out of the back door in his underpants. Cue for joke – I didn't know that you could have a back door in underpants but you know what I mean! Chris was also a songwriter and many moons later he wrote a chart hit for Cliff Richard – *My Kinda Life*. This was a hit in 1977 and the single had some great 'Dobro' slide guitar from a young gentleman by the name of Mo Witham! *My Kinda Life* was recorded with some great musicians. Alan Jones of 'The Shadows' was on bass, Roger Pope was the drummer, Alan Hawkshaw (also a 'Shadow' at one time) played the piano and well-known session vocalists Tony Rivers and John Perry did the backing vocals. Bruce Welch produced the track so there were three 'Shadows' connections! Mo even appeared with Sir Cliff (or plain Cliff as he was then) on 'Top of the Pops.' There were some good close ups of Mo's hands and you could see the tattoos on his fingers that were rumoured to have lost him the opportunity of joining Lulu's band 'The Luvvers' when they decided that the tattoos would not fit in with their (presumably) squeaky clean image.

Even though Mickey liked the name Jumping G Hosaphat common sense prevailed and the LP came out under the name 'Legend.' The 'Bell' LP came to the attention of David Knights who was the original bass player for 'Procol Harum' and who was thinking of leaving the band to go into management of other artists. There were existing connections between Mickey, 'The Shades' and 'Procol Harum 'as the 'Commander' of the band was (and is) Gary Brooker (formerly with 'The Paramounts.')

Gary had by now recruited Barrie (B J) Wilson and Robin Trower to play in 'Procol Harum', both ex-'Paramounts' as the new drummer and guitarist following the monster international success of *A Whiter Shade Of Pale*. David Knights had suggested that Mickey should record something a little more in the Rock and Roll/R&B vein than the 'Bell' album so he cut a bruising version of his own song, *Georgia George Pt 1.* (The story in this song is very much in the local guitarist makes good (Johnny B Goode!) vein.) I was asked if I wanted to be on this record but at the time I was still convinced that playing in a covers band and working at a sane day job would be better financially. (It was, but it was not nearly as much fun.) The Mickey Jupp penned record did feature Mo Witham and was produced by Robin Trower, with Matthew Fisher on bass and B J Wilson on drums. This single is described on 'Procol Harum's website as one of the most collectable singles for Procoholics. It was the first recording that had been produced by Robin Trower and was also the first time that Matthew Fisher had played bass on record. B J Wilson and Matthew did not play on record together again until 1985 when they appeared on Gary Brooker's excellent album *Echoes In The Night.* After one album and one gig Mickey broke up the first acoustic version of 'Legend' and through David Knights, his new manager, he approached Matthew Fisher and B J Wilson to record *Georgia George* with Mo on lead guitar.

David Knights was a charming man who had a quietly persuasive manner. He tended to wear a dark coloured velvet jacket with the nipped in waist that was so fashionable at that time and was altogether a real gent. In August 1969, David Knights and Mickey persuaded me to join a new version of 'Legend' with Mo on guitar and a guy called Bill Fifield on drums. One of our first gigs was at a roller skating rink on Pier Hill in Southend. This new meatier version of 'Legend' (compared to the more gentle acoustic line up) instantly clicked and it was a tight, sweaty band with a very good understanding of our chosen metier, yes – Rock and Roll again. Other early gigs for this new version of 'Legend' were also low key and included places like 'Rettendon Parish Hall' and 'Jubilee Hall' in Maldon. When we played at 'Jubilee Hall' we went to a local hostelry to get a drink and they refused to serve us because Bill's hair was too long. We did manage to imbibe elsewhere but on the way back Bill couldn't resist leaning into the doorway of the first pub and shouting: "Watch out! Jesus is on the way in and he's got long hair!" Bill was another gentle kind of person so it was astounding to see him playing drums with huge thick sticks that looked like small tree trunks. He was also a great worrier and being a sensitive sort of chap he sometimes took to heart the rough banter that always goes on between musicians. He was a rock steady drummer and played in a deceptively simple style that underpinned the dual guitars that Mickey and Mo often played with some interesting and effective cross-riffing going on.

Mickey continued to play piano for at least part of the evening and was still using steam pianos and we sometimes found that the house pianos were in poor states of repair and they were usually hopelessly out of tune. Mickey carried his trusty pliers everywhere and wherever possible he tuned up the worst strings or even snipped out ones that would not budge. It was quite possible to hear a run down played on the piano by Mickey that had the odd silent note because the string had been cut by our resident piano tuner. I had by now purchased another of those huge 'Selmer Goliaths', as I had sold my old pair of these beasts when I left 'The Fingers.' I later teamed it up with a 'Sound City' 4 X 12 cabinet and the extra top that it contributed to the sound was quite welcome. The 'Sound City' cab was however, only an 80-watt unit so despite its size it was not very powerful. David Knights had lent me his 'Marshall' 100-watt bass amp so, compared to the 'Selmer Treble and Bass 50' I was now quite capable of being a noisy bastard. The 'Marshall' amp was a staple part of bass players' armoury at that time and had a punchy sound. We were encouraged by David to think about the clothes that we wore on stage and we couldn't decide what to wear as this seemed to us to be much less important than the music. We plumped for black shirts, black trousers and white scarves, tied Pikey style round our necks.

We were soon playing regularly at 'The Cricketers' Inn' ('The Cricketers' again – now 'The Riga Music Bar.') 'The Cricketers' had a section of the building where there were stairs going up to the toilets and a hanging balcony round the outside of the first floor. Many strange items were thrown down into the crowd from the balcony and one night there was even an enthusiastic sexual display on the dance floor by a couple that was cheered on by the friendly crowd, viewing the entire proceedings from the balcony and all round the fumbling erotic athletes.

Rehearsals were often held at 'The Cricketers' in the same room that we recorded *I'm Just A Drifter* with George Bird. This room had the added advantage of having a mini-piano in it. We soon started to take this piano on outside gigs due to the kind permission extended to us by Freddie Spring, who was the landlord and who loved our music. His son (another Freddie) is still the landlord to this day. One of the potmen at 'The Cricketers' perfected a soulful cry that he would repeat at various intervals at closing time. Frank would say; 'Come along now. Ain't you got no homes to go to?'

'Legend' started to do more and more colleges and universities and one of the first that we did was at 'Barking College', where we supported 'The Keef Hartley Big Band' and 'Daddy Longlegs.' 'The Keef Hartley Big Band' was a tight and punchy thirteen-piece band including drummer and leader Keef Hartley and an excellent guitarist called Miller Anderson. They made eight albums and four singles, all for 'Deram' between 1969 and 1974. Hartley came form Preston and was the drummer that replaced Ringo Starr in 'Rory Storm and The Hurricanes.' He was in 'The Artwoods' and then he played for John Mayall. 'The Big Band' was formed in 1968. Keef and Miller were also to play with each other again in 'Dogsoldier' but this band did not last for too long.

'Daddy Longlegs' had a shifting personnel but their first line up was: Moe Armstrong, Clif Carrison, Steve Hayton, Stephen Miller and Kurt Palomaki on vocals, drums, guitar, keyboards and bass respectively. They made four albums. (One was on 'Warner', another was on 'Vertigo' and the final two were on 'Polydor.') Their albums were issued between 1970 and 1972 and featured music that was rock/blues with a country influence.

Another example of a fairly early college gig was the night that we played with 'Taste' and 'The Climax Chicago Blues Band' at Bromley Tech. 'Taste' was a trio led by the brilliant blues guitarist Rory Gallagher (RIP). Rory was born in Ireland in1948. He took up the guitar at the age of 9 and by 13 he had formed his first band. When he was 16 he joined 'The Fontana Showband' (which became 'The Impact') and it was with this band that he toured in Britain in 1964. In 1965 Rory formed a trio with the bassist from 'The Impacts' and a drummer with whom he played in Germany. In 1966 he formed 'Taste' with Eric Kitteringham (bass) and Norman Damery (drums). He revamped the line-up in 1968 to include Richard McCracken (bass) and John Wilson (drums). 'Taste' upped sticks to London in 1968 and played in Germany again. 1969 saw them touring the US and Canada supporting 'Blind Faith.' 'Taste' made their final appearance at the Isle of Wight Festival in 1970. After 'Taste' split up Rory went solo and had various line ups in his new backing group over the years. His album *Live! In Europe* earned Rory platinum sales in 1972 and he was also named as Melody Maker's 'Musician of the Year' in that same year. In late 1994 Rory fell seriously ill while touring in Europe and he died on 14th June, 1995 in King's College Hospital, London, from complications following a liver transplant in April.

'The Climax Chicago Blues Band' came from Stafford and

was formed in 1967. Their vocalist/saxist was Colin Cooper and he lined up guitarists Pete Haycock and Derek Holt, bassist Richard Jones, keyboardist Arthur Wood, and drummer George Newsome for this new band. Their first (self-titled) album came out in 1968 on Parlophone. Another LP was released in1969 and this was called *Plays On*. Jones had left the band in between the first two albums so Holt switched to bass. They also trimmed their name down in 1968 to 'The Climax Blues Band.' Their next album in 1970 was more in the rock vein (*A Lot Of Bottle* on Harvest Records.) *Tightly Knit* was their 1971 offering and at that stage drummer George Newsome left. John Holt later replaced him. In '73, the group toured the States on the strength of their 1972 album, *Rich Man. FM Live* featured their 'new sound' (alleged to be similar to 'Humble Pie') and this LP saw them as a four piece without Arthur Wood who left in '72. In 1976 they issued *Gold Plated*, which was their best seller, and the single *Couldn't Get It Right,* which went to number three in 1977. *Flying The Flag* was released in 1980 and a single was also lifted from this LP. The track in question was *I Love You*, which was a number 12 chart hit in 1981. 1981's *Lucky For Some* featured former Deep Purple bassist Glenn Hughes on vocals as well as Nicky Hopkins on keyboards (who had been on the previous album too.). 1983's *Sample And Hold*, had sterling support from various sessioneers but with the onset of the dreaded synthesisers in the 80's they made fewer and fewer records. They are still playing together after all these years, with a new line up but a lot of stamina!

We played everywhere that would have us and became popular with the Teds and Rockers. One gig (or maybe it was two?) at 'The Roundhouse' in Chalk Farm (1st May 1970) had a huge line up including:

- Emperor Rosko
- Marty Wilde
- Bert Weedon
- Roy Young (the best act all night)
- 'The Wild Angels'
- Tommy Bruce
- Vince Eager
- Heinz
- Dave Travis
- 'Legend'
- Screaming Lord Sutch
- 'The Breakaways'
- Joe Brown

Emperor Rosko (real name Mike Pasternak) was a force to be reckoned with in the sixties and I first heard of him during his popular stint with 'Radio Caroline.' This was a pirate radio station broadcasting from a boat in off shore waters. He is very well known in other countries but sometimes uses other names such as 'Kaiser Rosko' in Germany, 'Le President' in France, and 'El Presidente' in South America. Rosko was (and is) a loud forceful DJ and it is difficult to concentrate on anything else when he is on the radio! Rosko also played a big part in the early days of 'BBC Radio 1' and he appeared on the famous 'Radio Luxembourg.' 'Radio Luxembourg' was at one time the only way to hear popular music for youngsters but the reception in the UK was awful. I remember listening to 'Radio Luxembourg' when I was supposed to be in bed asleep and they had a habit of playing part of a record and fading the track, so between the weak signal and the deliberate part played track it was hard to hear a whole song sometimes.

Marty Wilde was one of the original and most convincing of the early Rock and Roll singers in the UK. He still tours and is a great singer but he has an unfortunate and obvious toupee. He has good stage presence and a real depth to his voice and if he ditched the syrup it would make no difference at all to his appeal. An early version of his band, 'The Wild Cats' included such luminaries as Big Jim Sullivan, Liquorice Locking and Brian Bennett so he had the most famous session guitarist of all (Big Jim) and two guys who later became part of 'The Shadows' (Liquorice and Brian.) Marty initially formed a band called 'Reg Smith and the Hound Dogs' and the group became popular at local gigs in the South of England. Reg (Marty) was offered some work as a solo singer in clubs in the West End and whilst there he was spotted by Larry Parnes (who was Tommy Steele's manager.) Larry Parnes signed Marty up with the blessing of his parents as he was still under age. Marty Wilde had thirteen consecutive hit records between1958 and 1962 and also gave the world the gorgeous Kim Wilde (his daughter) who had several hits many years later.

Bert Weedon started playing the guitar at twelve years old (just like me!) He later played with well-known bands such as 'The Ted Heath Band', Mantovani and 'The Squadronnaires'. Bert wrote a widely used guitar tutor called 'Play in a Day' which despite its hopelessly over optimistic title became a source of knowledge for many a young guitarist. He also had various hits and even recorded his own insipid version of *Apache*. Bert embraced the new Rock and Roll music when it started to seep over England and played on records for many of the new Rock and Roll stars such as Tommy Steele, Marty Wilde, Laurie London, Cliff Richard, Adam Faith and Billy Fury. He has always prided himself on being able to play in may styles and he has backed other stars such as Frank Sinatra, Tony Bennett, Rosemary Clooney, Nat King Cole and Judy Garland.

Roy Young really set the place aflame. He sang like a

mixture of Ray Charles and Little Richard and was a mean piano player too. He had been through a baptism of fire in Germany in the early sixties and was a founder member of 'The Beat Brothers' with Tony Sheridan and Ringo Starr. He played with various other bands in Germany and even played keyboards with 'The Beatles' at one time. When his contract with 'The Star Club' expired Roy Young returned to the UK and joined 'Cliff Bennett and The Rebel Rousers.' 'The Roy Young Band' was formed in the seventies and released many albums including a live session with Chuck Berry. Roy has recorded with artists such as David Bowie and Long John Baldry as well as issuing many other records in his own name.

'The Wild Angels' were formed in 1967. The original members were Mal Gray (vocals), Mitch Mitchell (bass), John Hawkins (lead guitar), Bob O'Connor (drums) and John Huggett (keyboards). John Huggett left and Pete Addison replaced him on rhythm guitar who in turn was replaced by Dave Jacobs (who played rhythm and some piano.) Bill Kingston also later replaced Jacobs on piano. In May 1968, 'Bill Haley & the Comets' and Duane Eddy came to play gigs at London's 'Royal Albert Hall' and 'The Sophia Gardens Ballroom' in Cardiff. 'The Wild Angels' were the support act. They were still playing Rock and Roll at the time that many other bands were experimenting with the comparatively weedy psychedelic music (including 'The Fingers.') Mal Gray was a good showman and had a dark brooding stage presence. Their first single was a new version of an Eddie Cochran song with a B-side written by their manager. Elkie Brooks was one of the backing singers on this song that was penned by her then husband Pete Gage (their then manager) who had formerly been a guitarist with Geno Washington. Mitch left the band and was replaced by Rod Cotter. 'The Wild Angels' released an album called *Live*

At The Revolution, which got into the budget-price album charts but they had less success with singles. They did however tour as the backing group for Gene Vincent's last British Tour. The next album sold well but then Rod left to be replaced by Keith Reed. Bob O'Connor also left and was replaced by Geoff Britton from 'East of Eden.' Mal left and Keith took lead vocals for a new album, which was well received by the critics and sold well too. The group had a number one hit in Sweden with *I Fought The Law*. The band was gradually becoming more of a 'poppy' band and Geoff left to join 'Wings.' Other members left until no original members remained. There are sometimes reunions at Teddy Boy weekenders.

Tommy Bruce had his first hit in summer 1960 with *Ain't Misbehavin'*. Tommy's voice was hoarse and different; as if he had gargled with broken glass. He was a refreshing counterbalance to the usual smooth and fairly characterless vocal styling of some of the other chart acts at the time. Unfortunately Tommy only had another two hits. His famous stage sign off was 'Now That's Rock and Roll.'

Vince Eager was a member of the 'Larry Parnes stable', along with Tommy Steele, Marty Wilde, Billy Fury and Joe Brown. His skiffle band 'The Vagabonds' had Brian 'Liquorice' Locking on bass and came second in the World Skiffle championships. After leaving Parnes Vince Eager was active in cabaret and pantomime and spent five years in the West End show 'Elvis.'

Heinz (Heinz Burt) died aged 57 in 2000 as a result of motor-neurone disease. He was one of Joe Meek's recording stars and played bass in 'The Tornados', a group that had a huge hit with "Telstar" in 1962. Joe Meek wanted Heinz to be a solo star and he did have one hit with *Just Like Eddie* in 1963. Heinz bleached his hair at Meek's suggestion but had a weak voice. There was even some speculation that his lead vocals were beefed up on some records by having another singer's voice added. In later years Heinz appeared on stage at 1960s pop revival shows. These included a 1992 Meek tribute concert, where he concluded with *Teenager In Love*.

Dave Travis was originally a country-folk-blues singer but did record some rockabilly tracks early in his career. Before he had recorded Dave toured around Finland as a model for a local clothing company and also sang with a dance orchestra. Dave has backed many original American rockabilly and Rock and Roll artists on their recordings and UK tours, including such legends as Carl Perkins, Carl Mann, Eddie Bond, Charlie Feathers, Buddy Knox, Johnny Carroll, Sonny Burgess, Hayden Thompson, and Charlie Gracie. Today, Dave Travis has a reissue-label called 'Stomper Time Records.' At the time of 'The Roundhouse' concerts he had a band called 'Bad River.'

Screaming Lord Sutch amazed the punters at 'The Roundhouse' by climbing on top of a grand piano and stomping around on its highly polished surface whilst swinging his mike around by the lead. He was a real character and had an act that was in some ways similar to that of Screaming Jay Hawkins i.e. based on horror films and humour. Leopard skins, large bullhorns and long black hair were his forte and he was carried on stage in a coffin. His band 'The Savages' had an ambulance instead of the usual group van. Screaming Jay Hawkins once appeared at 'The Studio Jazz Club' in Westcliff (near Southend) and his act was indeed similar in feel to that of Lord Sutch. There is a story that when Screaming Jay Hawkins played in theatres he would pay for shrivelled rubber bands to be thrown into the audience in the stalls from the balcony and that his helpers would at the same time whisper:

" Worms..." Sutch's band at one time included Ritchie

Blackmore on guitar (later of 'Deep Purple') and Matthew Fisher (organ) (later of 'Procol Harum.'). A top hat and a black cloak became his signature clothing and he carried out mock attacks on young girls with knives. I had my very own top hat at one time and I bought this in 'The Lanes' at Brighton before a gig. The other members of the band disapproved of the hat and they stamped on it in the van on the way home a few gigs later in order to prevent me from wearing it any longer! Another example of wanton destruction of my property by band members was the time that Bob made a flowerpot from a 'Force Five' record! Joe Meek produced Lord Sutch's first few records. In 1965 he formed his own 'National Teenage Party' and stood as a parliamentary candidate for Stratford-Upon-Avon but he later stood in all by-elections with his 'Monster Raving Loony Party.' Lord Sutch died in 1999.

'The Breakaways' were formed by three of 'The Vernons' Girls'; Betty Prescott, Margot Quantrell and Vicki Brown (RIP). Their first record (on Pye in 1962) was *He's A Rebel.* Although it was the same song as 'The Crystals' hit this was actually a cover of the original recording by Vikki Carr. 'The Breakaways' were heavily used by 'Pye' (and other labels) as backing singers. This work included sessions for artists such as Julie Grant and Joe Brown. They did many live shows as well as their studio and TV work, including appearances supporting well-known acts like Jet Harris, Little Richard and Sam Cooke. Margot's husband was Tony Newman (referred to elsewhere) the drummer of 'Sounds Incorporated.' Vicki left the group but returned later and another ex-'Vernons Girl' - Jean Ryder replaced Betty. In the middle sixties 'The Breakaways' were doing up to three sessions per day, seven days per week. Whilst they were sometimes in the studio with the artists, the acts that they were backing were often not there when they laid down the backing vocals. The Breakaways were on *Shout* with Lulu, *Anyone Who Had A Heart* with Cilla, *Downtown* with Petula Clark, *Stay Awhile* with Dusty Springfield, and more – all in 1964. In 1965 they appeared on Burt Bacharach's hit *Trains And Boats And Planes* and they also sang on 'The Walker Brothers' record *Make It Easy On Yourself.* In 1966 acts 'Ready Steady Go' ended its miming policy due to changes in Musicians' Union rules and acts then had to perform live. 'The Breakaways' became resident backing singers on the show. Jean left for a short period and her deputy was another ex-Vernons Girl, Anne Simmons. In 1967, they issued *Sacred Love*, which was a Mike Leander song, and he also produced and arranged the session. February 1968 saw 'The Breakaways' recording three of the entries for the British 'Song For Europe' heats. They also recorded songs for Cliff's film 'Two A Penny'. They sang BV's for Cliff Richard again when he came second in 'The Eurovision Song Contest' with the well known but awful song *Congratulations.* Cliff recorded a live album with 'The Breakaways' at 'The Talk Of The Town' (also in 1968) and this was also the year of their last single *Santo Domingo* on 'MCA.' In 1971 they returned to Eurovision as part of a quartet backing Clodagh Rodgers' entry *Jack In The Box.* The first half of seventies was busy for them but the name 'The Breakaways' had ceased to be used by mid-seventies.

Joe Brown was and is a multi-talented musician who can play many instruments. He has played for many other stars such as Johnny Cash, Gene Vincent and Eddie Cochran. On early package tours Joe Brown was a frequent stalwart and he appeared with Bill Haley, Jerry Lee Lewis, Little Richard & Chuck Berry as well as being supported on some shows by a young band called 'The Beatles.' He formed his group, 'Joe Brown & The Bruvvers' in 1960 and has had many hits, including a number one success with *A Picture Of You*. In the early seventies Joe had a band called 'Brown's Home Brew' in which his wife Vicki Brown (ex-'Vernons' Girl' and 'ex-Breakaway') was also a member. Sadly Vicki is no longer with us. 'Brown's Home Brew' recorded on 'Vertigo', the same label that issued the 'Legend' *Red Boot* and *Moonshine* albums. Joe Brown has also worked extensively in film, TV and theatre appearances over the years. He is still a busy and popular act and is also a talented songwriter. Rock and Roll is always well supported and Joe is a regular on the revival circuit. He is a tireless individual who does 200 shows a year!

Shortly after the Round House Rock and Roll special(s) David Knights asked us if we would back Billy Fury for a gig at 'The Country Club' in Belsize Park. We rehearsed with Billy in a room over a pub on the outskirts of London and found him to be an extremely friendly and pleasant man. He patiently went through his repertoire with us, including very well known hits of his like *Halfway To Paradise*. Billy Fury was born in 1940 and christened Ronald William (surname Wycherly). In the 1950's and 60's he was a member of the Larry Parnes 'stable.' He had recurrent health problems caused by rheumatic fever, which he first contracted in 1946. Larry Parnes thought that Ronald Wycherley was not a suitable name for a James Dean look-alike pop idol and renamed him Billy - after bandleader Billy Cotton - and Fury, to compensate for the singer's shyness. Billy Fury had many hits and specialised in romantic ballads. Billy also appeared in several films and was a horse, fast car and motorcycle fan. Billy Fury died in January 1983 after being found unconscious in his flat in Cavendish Avenue, St John's Wood. He apparently died in the ambulance. His heart weakness, caused by rheumatic fever, caused his death. His records are still hugely popular and he is remembered as a really nice fellow.

On the night of the gig we were all looking forward to playing with Billy, apart from Mickey who really didn't want to back anybody else even if he was as well established and as popular as Billy Fury. The performance was very successful even though Mickey was playing snatches of *Rock Island Line* on the piano at the side of the stage when he should have been concentrating on the task of backing Billy; who was after all the person that the punters had paid to see. Billy later asked us if we wanted to be his permanent backing band but we turned this opportunity down so we could concentrate on 'Legend.'

One place 'Legend' played at regularly at that time was a club called 'The Pheasantry' in King's Road, Chelsea where the bar was upstairs and the bands played in a basement. The DJ there was a Scottish guy called Alex and we became quite friendly with him even though we usually regarded DJ's as parasites. Playing at 'The Pheasantry' involved us getting home to our beds in Southend at 5 30 in the morning. Many a time we froze in a smelly van leaning on speaker cabinets, or if you were very lucky you managed to get a seat next to the roadie, which was marginally more comfortable.

With eyes like piss holes in the snow, tired out and grumpy we agreed that to do this we must be Bark Staving Ronkers. I was working for a Lloyd's Insurance Broker as my 'day job' and my routine involved getting to bed as late as 5 30 or even 6 00 in the morning and getting up after only an hour or so's sleep, a quick bath and then into work by about 9 00.

In May 1970 we did a gig at 'The Hendon Classic' with a bill that was to have included Jimmy Ruffin but Bob and Marcia who sang their insidious hit *Young Gifted And Black* replaced him. Bob (Andy) and (Marcia) Griffiths' version of Nina Simone's *Young, Gifted And Black*, sold 1/2 million in the UK and Europe. They appeared on 'Top of the Pops' and toured extensively. They had another UK Top Ten single called *Pied Piper* and issued two albums for 'Trojan Records.' Marcia Griffiths had her first number one in Jamaica in 1968 with *Feel Like Jumping*. Although they toured extensively at the time there was little financial reward and so they returned to Jamaica. Marcia became one of Bob Marley's backing singers in 1975 and stayed with him into the '80's. After Bob Marley died in 1981, Marcia began to record more extensively and had a hit with Bunny Wailer in the USA in 1989 with *Electric Boogie*. This was seven years after it was recorded. She still records to this day. Bob Andy made solo records in the early '70's including a song called *Life* (not the Mickey Jupp song.) He has also spent time as an A & R man and released a Bob and Marcia album (*Really Together*) on his own label. Bob also dabbled in acting for five years but was back in the reggae charts in 1983 before returning to A & R work in 1987. Bob had itchy feet and went on tour again to Oz and Poland in 1989. He has appeared since then in Europe, Japan, Jamaica, Canada and the USA. He now lives in Florida.

The other turns were 'Marmalade' (a very good Scottish band who had several hits like *Rainbow*) and of course 'Legend' all introduced by Tony Blackburn. 'Marmalade' started life as 'The Gaylords' in 1961 but the first line up of 'Marmalade' (from 1963?) had Junior Campbell on lead guitar and keyboards, Raymond Duffy on drums, Pat Fairley on guitar, the aforesaid Dean Ford on lead vocals, and Graham Knight on bass. In 1966, Raymond Duffy went and a new drummer, Alan Whitehead replaced him. Hugh Nicholson from 'The Poets' replaced Junior Campbell in 1970. By 1971 Dougie Henderson (another Poet) came in on drums instead of Whitehead. In '72 Pat Fairlie left and then Nicholson departed. Confused yet? The line up by now was: Dean Ford (vocals), Graham Knight (bass), Dougie Henderson and new boy Mike Japp (guitar, keyboards and vocals.) (Mike Japp was one of the featured musicians on one of Matthew Fisher's solo albums.) Next to go was Graham Knight but he was soon back with a new version of 'Marmalade' with Alan Whitehead (drums), Sandy Newman (guitar, keyboards, vocals) and Charlie Smith (guitar.) The last movement that I can find was when Whitehead went (again) and Charlie Smith switched to drums. His guitar role was taken over by Alan Holmes who also plays keyboards and sings. 'The Gaylords' originally did soul and Tamla Motown covers. In 1967 they signed to CBS as 'Marmalade.' They were a good poppy band and their debut release as 'Marmalade' was *It's All Leading Up To Saturday Night*. They had another three releases before their breakthrough with *Lovin' Things*. They stuck to the commercial slant with *Wait For Me Mary-Anne* and a cover of 'The Beatles' song *Ob La Di* that was a No 1 smash. *Baby Make It Soon* was another Top 10 hit, but *Butterfly* was not a success and neither was the album, *There's A Lot Of It About*. They moved to 'Decca' and soon issued *Reflections Of My Life* written by Junior Campbell and Dean Ford. This was a hit in the UK and the States. They had four more hits with *Cousin Norman, Back On The Road, Radancer* and *Falling Apart At The Seams.*" Other recordings disappeared without a trace. Nonetheless 'Marmalade' are still touring and they are popular on the sixties revival circuit.

Tony Blackburn was born in 1943 and he made his first radio appearance in 1964 on 'Radio Caroline South.' He joined 'Radio London' in 1966. He was a regular on the 'BBC Light Programme' from 1967. He was also the very first DJ to appear on 'BBC Radio 1' in September 1967. Tony now presents a soul show for 'Jazz FM' and 'The Real Radio' group and also does a breakfast show for 'The Classic Gold Network.' He has many awards and also does a variety of TV work. Tony was a compere of the BBC's show 'Top of the Pops' from the late sixties and throughout the seventies. When he appeared in 'I'm a Celebrity ... Get me Out of Here!' in 2002 he was crowned King of the Jungle. On the night that we played at 'The Classic' in Hendon Tony made some well meaning but awful jokes (no change there then) about trying to get Frank Sinatra to appear there that night.

21.
Legend And The "Red Boot" On Vertigo

Legend' recorded an album at around that time that was produced by the famous Tony Visconti (who was also playing bass at the time with 'David Bowie and the Spiders from Mars') Tony Visconti played the ukulele at 5 with the help of some tuition from his father but later started to play guitar and at 13 he joined his first band, 'Mike Dee and the Dukes.' Later on Tony joined his high school's orchestra and brass band where he learned double bass and tuba respectively. When Tony left High school he joined (as bassist and guitarist) a Latin American band called 'Ricardo and The Latineers.' Tony did some night school to catch up on his High school 'gap' as he had left rather early; and then worked the night club scene all over New York. Tony has worked with many and varied musicians but his emergence on the Rock scene began after what he describes as 'a year on acid.' Tony and his wife Siegrid then joined the 'Richmond Organization' (publishing) and 'RCA' (recording.) After a while Tony was offered the job of 'house' record producer for the 'Richmond Organisation' and he accepted this job, little knowing how good a move this really was. At about this time Tony met Denny Cordell (the producer of Procol Harum's *A Whiter Shade Of Pale*. Tony blagged a chance of playing bass on a Denny Cordell produced session for Georgie Fame and he then started a new phase in his career! It was not long before Tony was working with Denny

Laine, 'Manfred Mann', Brian Jones, Georgie Fame, 'Procol Harum' and 'The Move.' Tony has been associated with great artists such as David Bowie, 'Thin Lizzy', 'T Rex', 'The Moody Blues', 'Gentle Giant' (another 'Vertigo' act) and many others. Tony was an amiable and very knowledgeable American who really knew his stuff. Therefore the best that we could have done would have been to let him have his head and for him to decide what mix to use, the right sounds and whether or not to use echo or reverb on the recordings. Mickey Jupp hates echo and reverb on vocals and insisted that the whole album should be recorded totally dry. This eventually made the resulting takes sound rather dull and lifeless so Tony retrospectively added echo to our efforts. This album now changes hands for ridiculous sums of money and is known as the *Red Boot* album because of the cover artwork, which shows a red, buckled, winkle picker boot on fire.

'Disc & Music Echo' carried quite a log review of the *Red Boot* LP:

'Legend take you completely by surprise, the nearest hint the album cover gives you to what to expect is a flaming, pointed toe and brass buckled boot. They're a bit difficult to explain: The influence and approach to the songs, all new ones by Mickey Jupp are without doubt rock-n-roll influenced but the influence is so far back as to be country tinged. The issue isn't forced. Noone strains vocal chords to sound like someone else, and if the rock-n-roll approach isn't right they don't seem to be bound by any purist shackles and use whatever is right. By the way, its an enjoyable album which is great fun, and we defy anyone to sat it's a carbon copy of the heroes of the golden fifties." The *Red Boot* album was recorded at 'Advision', which was at that time a famous studio. Many popular groups, such as 'Yes' and 'Emerson Lake and Palmer' have recorded there as well as solo artists like Paul Young and David Essex.

The *Red Boot* engineer was Eddie Offord who has worked with 'Emerson Lake and Palmer' and 'Yes' so he was no slouch either. Altogether, then we should have come out of these sessions with a respectable sounding LP but at the time we were not totally satisfied with our work. One day we arrived at the studio just as Keith Emerson (of 'ELP') was playing a complicated piece on a harpsichord. Now Keith is a very talented muso but this was not our style and we found 'ELP's' music to be over blown and pretentious. Keith finished his piece with a coda utilising fast and tricky finger work and this was accompanied by a huge and deliberately timed fart from Mo.

Mike Hugg, from 'Manfred Mann' had left a huge 'Moog Synthesiser' at 'Advision' and we couldn't resist experimenting with this beast, which was the grandparent of the digital keyboards that have now become so prevalent.

Robert Moog also invented the 'Theremin' that was used so effectively in the chorus of *Good Vibrations* by 'The Beach Boys.' Moog hit upon the idea of the idea of building new circuits for sound production in 1963. By 1964 he started to manufacture electronic music synthesisers. His synthesisers were designed in collaboration with the composers Herbert A. Deutsch, and Walter (later Wendy) Carlos. Before too long 'The Beatles' bought a 'Moog Synthesiser' and so did Mick Jagger.

We decided we rather liked the sound that we found and used it briefly on one track of the *Red Boot* album – so thanks Mike! A great part of the *Red Boot* album was recorded whilst we were totally pissed. David Knights would very kindly leave bottles of Teacher's Whiskey for us together with cans of coke. We had no glasses so the drill was to drink a small amount of coke out of the can and then to top up the can with a measure of whiskey. Of course as the can became more and more depleted of coke the whiskey to coke ratio tipped alarmingly in favour of the whiskey as we carried on topping up the can. It's surprising that the album came out as well as it did!

On one occasion we 'found' a stopwatch in the studio and on the way home we decided to use it to see how long it would take us to drive for 20 seconds. Guess what, it took us exactly 20 seconds!

It's a well known fact that the constant repetition of a number over and over again whilst recording can cause an artist to become fed up with the songs, the recording and the way that he has performed the eventual take. Listening to the album now I can enjoy it more than I did back then and the songs (all penned by Mickey) are still good. The overall feel was (slightly) updated Rock and Roll with some more poppy numbers a la 'Coasters' chucked in for good measure.

Two songs that didn't feature on the album were released as a single on the famous 'Vertigo' label in 1971. This featured a swirling black and white pattern on the record label and 'Vertigo' also the stable for some good acts such as 'Toe Fat', 'Gentle Giant' and 'Patto.'

The songs on that single were *Life* (a moody and dark rock ballad) backed with *Late Last Night* (a simple 12 bar blues.) *Life* was fairly successful in Italy later on but that is a whole different story!

In April 1970 we were asked to do a 'BBC2' TV show called 'Disco 2.' This was the forerunner of 'The Old Grey Whistle Test' and was introduced by Tommy Vance. 'Ten Years After' and 'Slade' were also on the same show as was Santana.

Tommy Vance (RIP) changed his name from Rick West by accident. An American radio station had taken on a DJ called Tommy Vance and had produced promotional material including the jingles before the 'real' Tommy Vance changed his mind. Rick West appeared instead and became Tommy Vance. Since that strange genesis Tommy has worked on 'Radio Caroline', 'Radio London' and other stations and was a well known presenter on 'Top of the Pops.'

'Slade' was one of the featured bands on the show that we were on and this was around the time that they were still sporting skinhead haircuts. Dave Hill and Don Powell had a band called 'The Vendors' in 1964 but in 1965 they became 'The N'Betweens' and issued records in France. At the time Noddy Holder was still working with Steve Brett who was a 'Columbia' artist. In 1966 Noddy left Steve Brett and became a road manager for 'Listen', who had Robert Plant as a singer. Noddy and Jim Lea talked about forming a band with Dave Hill and Don Powell and in late 1966 they became the next version of 'The N'Betweens'. At one stage Robert Plant was a possible vocalist but Noddy Holder took the position and they recorded *You Better Run* for 'Columbia.' The band was a covers group playing Motown, Beatles, Stax and ska on the Midlands club circuit but in 1969 they came to the smoke.

Their new name was 'Ambrose Slade' and Chas Chandler took them on. Chas Chandler was the ex-'Animals' bassist and later manager of Jimi Hendrix. He was also another 'Epiphone Rivoli' user like yours truly. 'Ambrose Slade' had quite a following amongst the 'skinheads' who back in those days were a relatively harmless lot compared to the version that exists nowadays. In the early 70s they loved reggae and ska. It was in 1970 that the band changed its name to Slade and they released two unsuccessful singles and an album called *Play It Loud*. In 1971 they had their first chart hit with *Get Down And Get With It* followed by, *Coz I Luv You*, which topped the European, charts. 'Slade' had six number ones and other successes over a five-year period. Holder and Lea wrote all their hits. A live album (surprisingly titled *Slade Alive!*) was issued in 1972 and reached number 2 and stayed there for over a year. They continued their trademark of strangely spelled records with their hits *Take Me Bak 'Ome* and *Mama Weer All Crazee Now. Gudbuy T' Jane* got to number 2 behind Chuck Berry's worst record, *My Ding A Ling.* 'Slade' continued their success and then released the archetypal Christmas record *Merry Christmas Everybody* which is still played every Christmas and drives Jim Lea mad as he says that the record is played too early every year! However, it sold a quarter million copies in its first day of release and was their biggest single. It was also immensely successful in Europe and re-charted every Christmas from 1981 – 1994.

'Ten Years After' had one of the original guitar heroes, Alvin Lee. He was born in 1944 and started to play locally at 13. 'Ten Years After' were originally called 'The Jaybirds' and were formed in 1965. The newly tagged quartet of Alvin Lee (guitar, vocals), Chick Churchill (keyboards), Ric Lee (drums) and Leo Lyons (bass) played a mixture of rock 'n' roll and blues. Their debut album was not a success and they worked hard in the clubs to build up a following. A live album *Undead* was recorded at 'Klooks Kleek' club and proved that Alvin Lee was a force to be reckoned with. There was a feeling however that the band was becoming the Alvin Lee show but they persevered and apparently did more US tours than any other UK band. They appeared at the famous 'Woodstock' festival in 1969 and in the film thereof. Alvin Lee started to do solo ventures from 1973 but the band recorded in 1974 and toured in 1975. 'Ten Years After' issued four solid albums, which were all chart successes in both the UK and the USA. There have been two 'Ten Years After' reunions, one in 1989 and another in 1997.

'Legend's' numbers for 'Disco 2' were recorded separately however, and we didn't get to meet the other acts. We did *Life* (our first 'Legend' single on 'Vertigo'), which was totally unrepresentative of the type of numbers that we played on stage. These were always much more Rock and Roll influenced and we always included many of the old standards of the genre such as *Great Balls Of Fire* and *Kansas City*. However, we also played *Hole in my Pocket* from the *Red Boot* album, which was more like our stage act.

There were several good Rock and Roll revival bands touring at the time including a welsh outfit called 'Shakin' Stevens and the Sunsets.' Now this was some time before Shaky became successful in the charts and by the time he did so he had obviously had some coaching in on stage presentation that had given his act a new buzz. 'Shakin' Stevens' was born in Ely, Cardiff. He had his roots in Rock and Roll and he and his band, 'The Sunsets' turned pro' in 1969. They continued to appear together until 1977. Shaky was featured on pretty much the same circuit as 'Legend' in the UK but he also worked in Europe. Between 1970 and 1976 he and his band recorded albums and singles for various companies and they worked with Dave Edmunds as producer on one LP that was coincidentally named *A Legend*. 'Shakin Stevens' was very popular in Holland. He and his group were voted the Top Live Band of 1972 in the UK by 'New Musical Express' readers. *Jungle Rock,* a cover of a Hank Mizell song was the last recording made with 'The Sunsets' in 1976. Stevens signed up as a solo artist to 'Track Records' in mid-76 and released a single called *Never* in March 1977. This was not successful and in September 1977 he issued *Somebody Touched Me*. Again there was no chart recognition in the UK but it was a hit in Australia. In the autumn of 1977, Shakin Stevens was asked by veteran impresario Jack Good to appear in the West End musical about 'Elvis' and his performances in the show were exceptionally well received. 1978 saw a new single *Justine* and a self-titled LP. 'Track' folded and Shaky moved to 'Epic' in mid-1978. He put out three more singles on 'Epic' but none of them charted. He carried on with his successful role in 'Elvis' and then appeared in a new live version of 'Oh Boy' which prompted similar shows for TV. Stevens became even more successful in the early 1980's. His album *Take One* (1980) featured the incredible country rock guitarist Albert Lee. (Many years later Albert was to become one of 'Bill Wyman's Rhythm Kings' with Gary Brooker – ex-'Paramount.') *Hot Dog,* a single from the album was a hit in the same year and then there was another hit with *Marie, Marie* six months later. Shaky had his first number one in 1981 with *This Ole House,* which was very big internationally. There were two more number ones in 1981 and other hits too. Shaky also released two hit albums in that same year and wrote his own number one hit *Oh Julie,* which charted the following year. Shakin Stevens had more hits here and abroad right through the seventies and even the eighties.

'The Wild Angels' were also a good act that we played with fairly frequently. They had a singer called Mal Gray fronting this band that clearly loved the music they were playing. At a gig at 'The Roundhouse' Bert Weedon carefully explained to their lead guitar player that he could achieve a much clearer sound if he did so and so with his amp controls. To give him his credit the guy receiving the well-meaning advice thanked Bert very much for the tips even though it was quite clear from his preferred sound that a dirty Rock and Roll feel was what he was after!

I have some old publicity photos' that were taken at around this time and we did a shoot on board a replica of Sir Francis Drake's ship, the Golden Hind that used to be 'moored' next to the pier in Southend. Our friend French Henry owned this Golden Hind. (Shouldn't that be French Henri?)

Legend on The Golden Hind – 1971 (L to R)
Mo Witham, Mickey Jupp, Bill Fifield, John Bobin

Other gigs included a session at 'The 100 Club' in Oxford Street in May 1970. 'The 100 Club' started in 1942 and was originally a restaurant called 'Mack's' and which has carried several names over the years. The club was a jazz venue called 'The Feldman Club' at first but over the years it has featured many varied artists and diverse styles of music. Glen Miller appeared at the Club in its early days, with several members of his famous band. During the Second World War the club carried on bravely and adverts suggested that punters should 'Forget the Doodle bug-Come and Jitterbug at the Feldman club' In the late 40's it became 'The London Jazz Club' and featured jitterbug and swing music. In the 50's it carried the name 'The Humphrey Lyttleton Club' and in 1956 Louis Armstrong played at the club as well as Humphrey's own band and Chris Barber. Trad jazz was beginning to be popular and the club changed musical direction to follow this new craze during the late fifties and early sixties. Many other well-known Trad Jazz acts cam to the club such as Acker Bilk and Kenny Ball. After a spell as the 'Jazz Shows', the name 'The 100 Club' was then selected for another musical journey through the blues and R&B boom. Muddy Waters, Jimmy Rushing, Otis Spann and many others appeared including the owner of the strange shaped guitars, Bo Diddley. The British R&B groups included 'Steam Packet', Alexis Korner and 'John Mayall's Bluesbreakers' who all appeared at the 100 Club. Other bands that played there included 'The Who' and 'The Kinks.' The club also supported other musical crazes. Styles as far apart as Punk (with the infamous 'Sex Pistols') African jazz, and 'Indie' music have all been played at the club with a pedigree, 'The 100 Club.'

We also continued to do gigs at various Rocker strongholds such as 'The Northcote Arms' in Southall. The audience there was a tough mix of Rockers and Teds and it was not unknown for bottles to fly through the air and for either one to one scuffles to develop or at some times a rather grander melee to break out. Rather surprisingly we did not feel at all threatened in this environment as the punters had adopted us as 'their' band and were rather protective of us lads who were still on the young side compared to some of the customers. Other gigs at about this time included 'The Railway Hotel' in Wealdstone, 'The Kings' Arms' in Wood Green and 'The Mitre' (near Blackwall Tunnel.) We also played at 'The Barn Club' in Stansted, 'Colchester Corn Exchange' and 'La Grotta' on Southend seafront. Another and posher venue was 'Skindles Hotel' in Maidenhead. One of the roadies that was working for us at the time, Barry, was a bass player in a band called 'Iron Maiden' (not the well known one that surfaced later) and he supplemented his earnings with his band by working for us. He had very long hair but used to insist on greasing it up into a Rocker style every time we went to a Rocker haunt just in case he was picked upon for being a 'bloody hippy.'

'Legend' started to do more gigs at colleges and universities such as 'Brasenose College', 'Oxford Polytechnic' and 'Queen Elizabeth College' and we were lucky enough to appear on the same bill as many very famous acts —but more of that later.

One gig at 'Oxford Polytechnic was the night that we supported 'Audience.' The first line-up for 'Audience' was: Tony Connor (drums), Keith Gemell (woodwind), Howard Werth (guitar, vocals) and Trevor Williams (bass, keyboards and vocals.) They released five albums between 1969 and 1973 (although the '73 offering was a compilation.) 'Audience' also released three singles in 1971 and another in 1972. They were based in London and enjoyed some considerable popularity on the club and college circuit. 'Audience' toured in the States with 'The Faces' and built up a good cult following there. After 'Audience' split up, their members dispersed into various other ventures. For example Werth went to the US to join up with the surviving 'Doors' members but returned to the UK later. Connor joined 'Jackson Heights' and then 'Hot Chocolate.'

One of the agencies that we used at the time was indeed called 'College Entertainments.' They had some great acts for which they got bookings such as:

- 'The Peddlers'
- 'Magna Carta'
- Wild Wally
- 'Spirit of John Morgan'
- 'Jellybread'
- Jonathan Kelly
- 'Fairfield Parlour'
- 'Quatermass'
- 'CMU'
- 'Opal Butterfly'
- 'Barrow Poets'
- 'Help Yourself'
- 'Nashville Teens'

We use a fair few agencies but as the dealings with these agencies were always with David Knights I don't know why we shifted allegiance so many times or maybe we just worked with various agents simultaneously?

Another of these agents was 'Northern Music (incorporating Thumpers.)' They booked out a varied set of acts including:

- 'Fairfield Parlour'
- 'Czar'
- 'Marsupilami'
- 'Stackwaddy'
- Duffy Power (who had been backed on one of his singles by 'The Paramounts')
- 'The Purple Gang'
- 'Velvet Opera'

- Mike Absalom
- 'Affinity'
- 'Nirvana' (a 'Vertigo' band, not the Kurt Cobain group)
- Rosetta Hightower

A momentous event occurred one evening at a venue on 'Eel Pie Island.' This was my first ever sighting of an attractive young girl wearing a see through blouse with no bra! The way she flaunted herself left us in no doubt that she was positively enjoying the sexual frisson that she was causing. The place was also cold and damp and her nipples were an outstanding joy to behold! (Or should I say two outstanding joys?) Whilst Merseybeat was girding its loins in Liverpool in the early 1960s R&B was beginning to be played in London and a run down hotel on 'Eel Pie Island' was the unlikely venue that played a big part it is emergence. The hotel was popular in the 19th century and later ran tea dances during the 1920's and 1930's. In the mid-fifties a junk-shop owner started to hold dances at 'Eel Pie Island' using jazz acts like Ken Colyer and George Melly.' Eel Pie Island' had a big part to play as a catalyst for the sixties R&B rejuvenation and featured many great acts between 1962 and 1967. These included 'Cyril Davies' Rhythm & Blues All Stars', 'Long John Baldry's Hoochie Coochie Men' (with Rod Stewart), 'John Mayall's Bluesbreakers' (featuring Eric Clapton) and 'The Downliners Sect.' In 1967 (the summer of love!), 'Eel Pie Island' closed because the repairs that were needed became just too expensive to bear for the owner and soon the only appearances there were by squatters. In 1969, the Club opened again as 'Colonel Barefoot's Rock Garden' and progressive bands like 'The Edgar Broughton Band' appeared. After a demolition order, the hotel burnt down in 1971.

Back in the mid sixties Ricky. Dave and myself used to go

to the famous club 'The Marquee' every Wednesday night to see 'The Spencer Davis Group' with a very young but supremely talented Stevie Winwood on guitar and 'Hammond' organ. He had an amazing voice and I well remember him introducing their new single *Keep On Running*. I was thrilled therefore when 'Legend' appeared at 'The Marquee' on a special night promoted by 'Vertigo' for their acts, 'Dear Mr Tyme' and 'Legend. '

We also played at 'The Marquee' for a night called 'Sandham's Village' at which the acts were 'UFO', 'Little Free Rock', 'Root and Jenny Jackson's Peace Corps', 'Brewer's Droop', 'Balloon', 'Banana' and us!

'Little Free Rock' came from Preston in Lancashire and their line up was: Peter Illingworth, (lead guitar and vocals), Paul Varley, (drums) and Frank Newbold (bass and vocals.) They released an album in 1969 on the 'Transatlantic' label and also worked with 'Ginger Johnson's African Drummers 'as an Afro-Rock/Santana type band. (Ginger Johnson's Drummers had stimulated a great deal of interest in their act by appearing with 'The Rolling Stones' in a concert in Hyde Park during 1969.) The group performed at 'The Roundhouse' Sunday Night 'Implosion' gigs and played extensively on the Continent. The great blues guitarist, Peter Green, was a member of 'Little Free Rock' for a short time.

'Root and Jenny Jackson' were a Manchester based Ike and Tina turner style soul review band. Like many bands of the time they performed on the college, club and pub circuit. Root later led a band called 'FBI' ('Funky Bands Inc.')

'The Marquee Club's' programme at the time showed that they featured many well-known names (unfortunately on other nights) such as 'Yes', DJ Bob Harris, 'The Faces' and 'The Groundhogs.' Bob Harris later became a great supporter of Mickey and used to play his records on his BBC Radio shows.

'Juicy Lucy' was another 'Vertigo' band that we came across and the bass player/singer was Paul Williams who we first saw in 'Zoot Money's Big Roll Band' at a jazz club in Westcliff on Sea.) 'The Studio Jazz Club' was a smoky, friendly and busy club where 'The Orioles' sometimes played after already doing an earlier session at 'The Cricketers.' This practice (known as doubling) ensured that the band was busy and helped with cash but was very tiring. I well remember being at the club one day and waiting to join a jam session with Rob Trower, which had still not started well into the small hours. I just could not keep awake and had to go home to catch up on my badly needed beauty sleep. Rob told me the next day at 'The Shades' that he had decided to confiscate my 'Ravers badge!' The Studio did have some great acts appearing there such as John Lee Hooker (who had the catch phrase 'Boom Boom' before Basil Brush) and Screaming Jay Hawkins.

Some of the college and university balls were quite elaborate and costly affairs. 'Brasenose College' goes back to 1509 and completely ignorant of its history 'Legend' played there in 1970 as part of a bill that included:
- 'The Idle Race' (with leader Jeff Lynne)
- 'Monty Python's Flying Circus' (Michael Palin, John Cleese and Terry Jones)

'The Idle Race' story goes back to the late fifties. A Birmingham band called 'Billy King and the Nightriders' was formed and after Billy King left they became 'Mike Sheridan and the Nightriders'. Norrie Paramor (a well known record producer and also a band member previously with my uncle Eric Ryan) thought that there might be a chance to cash in on Mersey Beat by promoting Brum Beat i.e. music of the same ilk but from Birmingham. Many bands converged at a local club for auditions and Mike and his band were asked to make a record. There were personnel changes along the way and a couple of unsuccessful singles. In 1964 they needed a new guitarist and he was the wonderful Roy Wood. Roy was very keen on harmonies and persuaded them to widen their repertoire. They even toyed with comedy routines including Roy's Dusty Springfield impersonation. Many bands of the time experimented with comedy, for example 'The Finger's did awful and not very funny impersonations of 'The Beverly Sisters' and 'Nina and Frederick.' Along the way 'The Nightriders' changed their name to 'Mike Sheridan's Lot' and continued to record what were unfortunately unsuccessful singles. Roy Wood left to join 'The Move' in 1966 and although he was replaced his successor had a tough job filling the massive gap left by Roy's departure. More personnel changes followed (and they also went back to being called 'The Nightriders.') Jeff Lynne (another supremely talented musician) joined in November 1966. Jeff used a violin sound on his guitar, a technique that was inherited from the guitarist he replaced. The band started to use original material and changed their name to 'The Idyll Race', which was soon changed again to 'The Idle Race.' 'The Idle Race' then signed to 'Liberty' and recorded a version of Roy Wood's, *Here We Go Round the Lemon Tree.* 'The Move' had by now started to have massive hits like *Flowers In The Rain* and they recorded their own version of *Here We Go...* and this was played a lot on the radio so 'The Idle Race' released a Jeff Lynne song instead. They were a very good band with varied influences. Kenny Everett once described the Idle Race as 'second only to the Beatles!' In 1970 Jeff Lynne left 'The Idle Race' to join 'The Move'. After he had gone two new musicians replaced him and a final album called *Time Is* was recorded in '71. 'The Idle Race' then split but in 1972 the remains of the group emerged as part of 'The Steve Gibbons Band' who still play together today.

'Monty Python's Flying Circus' was an insane and bizarre TV show that owed much to 'The Goons' in terns of inspiration. The show first appeared on the BBC in October 1969 and was a vehicle for zany and often completely pointless sketches by Graham Chapman (RIP), John Cleese, Terry Gilliam, Eric Idle, Terry Jones and Michael Palin. The final episode on the BBC was shown in December 1974. It ran for 45 episodes but the final six were Cleese-less and had become simply 'Monty Python.' It was a very popular show that spawned several books and films as well as foreign offerings. Most people who remember the show have favourite sketches such as the Dead Parrot sketch or the Ministry of Funny Walks. Some say 'Monty Python's Flying Circus' was John Cleese's finest hour but for my money 'Fawlty Towers' deserves that honour. The Monty Python guys were hilarious at 'Brasenose College' and they did perform many well-known sketches including the Dead Parrot routine.

We enjoyed those college gigs tremendously and it is still a surprise to me how places like 'Borough Road College' and other seats of learning were able to afford such high quality do's.

In September 1970 we played at 'Ronnie Scott's' famous club. Ronnie Scott and Pete King opened their jazz club in October 1959. The club was then housed in premises in Gerrard Street, in Soho. Scott had long dreamed of opening a club for jazz musicians and they founded a place where British jazzers could jam in an informal atmosphere. Their first act was 'The Tubby Hayes Quartet.' Ronnie Scott became well known for his dry wit and sarcastic sense of humour, which he used to devastating effect during his droll introductions for visiting acts. After a couple of years they succeeded in getting round previously unhelpful MU red tape and then started to book American musicians as well as home baked equivalents. Exchange deals had to be set up so 'The Tubby Hayes Quartet' went to New York and Zoot Sims came to Ronnie Scott's. Other stars that appeared included Johnny Griffin, Roland Kirk, Al Cohn, Stan Getz, Sonny Stitt, Benny Golson and Ben Webster. Many other class musicians also appeared at Scott's club such as Wes Montgomery, Freddie Hubbard, Donald Byrd and Art Farmer. In 1965 Ronnie Scott and Peter King moved the club to Frith Street with financial aid from top promoter Harold Davison. The Frith Street premises were extended in 1968 at which stage an upstairs room was added which is where 'Legend' appeared. The new improved club opened in October 1968 with Buddy Rich. The club has always had a penchant for booking a wide spread roster of acts and artists such as Tom Waits, Linda Lewis, Elkie Brooks, Eric Burdon, Paul Rodgers and Jack Bruce have played 'Ronnie Scott's.' In 1996. Ronnie Scott died. He had been unwell for two years. He had been unable to play sax following problems with his teeth and even when he tried to have implants there were unforeseen complications and he could not blow and practise. The press tittle-tattled as they do whenever there is any trouble but the coroner's verdict was death by misadventure.

Another place that we played at more frequently was 'The Revolution.' This was a very popular club that featured many well-known stars, both in the audience and on stage. A contemporary programme included Georgie Fame, 'Lindisfarne', 'Lfetime' (with Jack Bruce), 'Barclay James Harvest', 'Bob Kerr's Whoopee Band' and 'Airforce.' 'The Revolution' was the club where live clips of 'Cream' (the group that Jack Bruce had told me about in Ramsgate) were filmed for *Fresh Live Cream*. Many other well-known bands appeared there such as 'Genesis', 'Hawkwind', 'Supertramp' and 'Mud' so 'Legend' was in very god company.

'Blaises' was another of the well-known places and here they had acts like Ben E King! Jimi Hendrix also appeared at the club in 1966 at about the time that 'The Fingers' were first toying with early recordings. 'Family' also played at 'Blaises.'

'The Pheasantry' in King's Road was a club with attitude and a history. It was once a drinking club and Dylan Thomas was a frequent visitor. Singer Yvonne Elliman moved to London in 1969 and Andrew Lloyd Webber and Tim Rice discovered her whilst she was singing at 'The Pheasantry.' She went on to play Mary Magdalene in their new rock opera, 'Jesus Christ Superstar.' Serafina Astafieva, the famous ballerina, once owned 'The Pheasantry' (well before it became an artists' gathering place.) The practice barre still remains on the first floor and there is now a large terrace courtyard and sweeping entrance. Renovations cost almost £1 million, but the pizza restaurant, which it has now become, rakes in the money! Eric Clapton once also shared a flat with the artists Martin Sharp and Phillipe Mora at 'The Pheasantry.' 'The Pheasantry' was at one time a rather grand house and somehow it became a gathering place for diverse intellectuals and arty types such as George Harrison, psychiatrist R.D. Laing, and Germaine Greer.

We also gigged at 'The Angelique' (another Chelsea club) and 'Sisters' (in Seven Sisters Road) plus other venues like 'The Two J's Club' in Braintree and 'Letchworth Youth Centre.' We even did an 'Old Tyme Fayre' at 'South Molton Assembly Rooms' although I can't see how a fifties/early sixties style band can really be referred to as 'Old Tyme.'

We supported 'Renaissance' one night at a club called 'The Granary.' 'Renaissance' was another band that did the Hokey Cokey with band members but their first line up was: Louis Cennamo (bass), John Hawken, (keyboards), Jim McCarty (drums), Jane Relf (vocals) and Keith Relf (guitar, vocals, harmonica.) They released seven albums and one single up to 1976. Their first two albums and a single were on 'Island' and albums three and four were issued by 'Sovereign'. LP's five, six and seven were on the 'BTM' label.

Keith Relf was the ex-'Yardbirds' singer/harp player and their drummer Jim McCarty had also worked with Keith in 'The Yardbirds'. 'Renaissance' was formed in 1969. They tried to fuse classical, folk, jazz, blues and rock music with their first self-titled LP. Relf and McCarty left before the second album *Illusion,* which was recorded for 'Island' but not released at the time. The next outing, *Prologue* was more popular in America than it was here and the band based them selves in the USA for a time. They had also acquired new talent in Annie Haslam who had a clarity and purity to her voice that had to be heard to be believed. The next two albums are generally thought to be their best. (*Turn Of The Cards* and *Scheherazade And Other Stories.*) In 1978 *A Song For All Seasons* became their best selling UK album, reaching No 35 in the charts. The hit single, *Northern Lights*, which got to No 10 in the UK came from this LP. They continued to record into the eighties.

The colleges sometimes had themed rag balls and one was a Medieval Masque styled night at the 'Charles Morris Summer Night Revels.' At this function 'The Wild Angels' played, as did Alan Elsdon with his fine trad jazz band. At around that time, Alan Elsdon was a well-known and hard working bandleader. His band was used for gigs, recording, films, and TV and worked extensively. He was a contemporary of many of the great trad jazz musicians such as Ken Colyer, Terry Lightfoot, Mike Daniels, George Melly and Humphrey Lyttleton.

Many of the clubs had sophisticated sounding names e.g. 'The Scotch of St James' where we also appeared. 'The Scotch of St James' had many stars as visitors. These included P.J. Proby, John Lennon, Jess Conrad, David Hamilton, Olivia Newton John and Bruce Welch. 'The Scotch of St. James' is now 'The Directors' Lodge Club' and was located next to the 'Indica Gallery'. John Lennon met Yoko Ono at this gallery in 1966. In the same year Jimi Hendrix played at the club with 'The VIP's.' 'The Jimi Hendrix Experience' made their London debut at the 'Scotch of St. James' shortly thereafter.

The 'Legend' single *Life* had a few radio plays on shows such as:

- Radio One club
- Johnny Walker show
- Emperor Rosko
- Top Gear (John Peel)

Life was reviewed in Disc and Music Echo and this what they said about it: 'Just like the sort of slow pumping rock ballads Conway Twitty used to do so well only here the words actually mean something. Great piano and vocals from leader Jupp.'

'Legend' was being booked out by an agency called 'Trigrad' and they had at least three 'Vertigo' acts on their lists, which were:

- 'May Blitz'
- 'Patto'
- 'Legend'

They also had other acts too and I believe it was they that got us the Billy Fury gig.

We also did quite a few live radio dates and I kept details of the songs that we performed:

- **Radio 1 Club 03/02/1971**

Cheque Book

Lorraine Pt 1

Great Balls Of Fire*
Treat Me Nice*
Further On Up The Road*
Don't You Never
• **Top Gear** 13/03/1971
It Hurts Me Too*
Don't You Never
Further On Up The Road*
I Can't Lose*
• **Radio 1 Club 20/03/1971**
*Treat Me Nice**
• **Radio 1 Club 30/03/1971**
Cheque Book
*Rockin' Pneumonia And The Boogie Woogie Flu**
• **Radio 1 Club 31/03/1971**
Don't You Never
• **Radio 1 Club 01/04/1971**
Don't You Never
• **Radio 1 Club 02/04/1971**
Cheque Book
• **Radio 1 Club 26/04/1971 - 30/04/1971**
Above six tracks repeated
• **Johnny Walker Show**
Above six tracks repeated (twice)
03/05/1971 - 07/05/1971 and
17/05/1971 - 21/05/1971
• **Top Gear 05/06/1971**
Lorraine Pt 1
*It Hurts Me Too**
*Further On Up The Road**
*I Can't Lose**
Shortly after this 'Legend' released a new single on 'Vertigo'

called *Don't You Never.* This song had a piano intro that just would not go right for Mickey who was becoming more and more grumpy until Tony Visconti suggested that the rest of us should head off down the pub and leave him and Mick to it. When we came back the deed was done and the result sounded fine. When *Don't You Never* came out it was coupled with a track that we had recorded at the time we laid down the *Red Boot* Album and this pleasant country flavoured track, *Someday*, although it had been left off the tracks selected for the *Red Boot* LP was a good example of how the band was able to turn its hand to many styles of music, not just Rock and Roll.

I had by now part-exchanged the bass that I had bought when I started to play again after my break, following my departure from 'The Fingers.' The bass that I ditched was a 'Gibson EB2' (effectively the same bass as the 'Epiphone Rivoli', which I sold when I left 'The Fingers'.) The 'Gibson' was more sought after than the 'Epiphone' equivalent but in all honesty they were not very different. I wanted to change to a 'Fender Precision', which as we all know was THE bass in the sixties and is still heavily used nowadays. Mickey hated it. He much preferred the muddy bassy sound of my old bass. Nonetheless I soldiered on and I still feel that the sound of the 'Fender' is miles better than the 'EB2.'

We were still playing at the colleges like 'Ravensbourne College of Art' in December 1970. At one gig where we played at a 'College of Law' we played with 'The Alan Bown Set' who played football with us and then pinched our football. This band was a soul and blues group and played regularly on the club circuit at the time that 'Legend' was still peddling Rock and Roll. They had some success with a single called *We Can Help You* in the late sixties, which reached number 26 in the 'NME' chart. They also covered *Headline News* (originally an

Edwin Starr number.) The band issued 12 singles and 4 albums on various different labels. Alan Bown was once a trumpeter with 'The John Barry Seven' (the outfit that originally featured guitar legend Vic Flick.) He formed his own 'Set' in 1965. They had various line ups; one of which was: Alan Bown (trumpet), Stan Haldane (bass), John Helliwell, (sax), Robert Palmer (RIP), (vocals), Vic Sweeny (drums.) They soon became favourites on the R&B and soul circuit. Later they changed their name to 'The Alan Bown!' The singer at the time that 'Legend' played with them was Jess Roden. Alan Bown joined 'CBS' as an 'A & R' man in 1974.

This gig also had a steel band. The colleges were always trying to do something different.

Bill Fifield had been playing on some sessions for Tony Visconti including records with Ralph MacTell and 'T Rex.' One of Bill's first sessions was on *Hot Love* and Marc Bolan asked him to join 'T Rex' after that session. Bill departed to spend three years or so with 'T Rex' and toured all over the world with Marc under the nom de drums of Bill Legend. Tony Visconti says: 'Bill and I had worked together when he was the drummer in the group 'Legend', a superb rock and roll group headed by Mickey Jupp, from Southend. Bill played great on *Hot Love* and Marc made him an offer he couldn't refuse.' The main man in 'T Rex' was of course Marc Bolan (RIP) whose real name was Marc Feld. Marc was born in 1947 and by the age of 12 he was in a band led 'Susie and The Hula Hoops.' Always a snappy dresser and a fashionable chap he even started to copy the mod clothes when he was 13. He was a young model for a short time but at 17 he went back to his first love, music and changed his name to Toby Tyler. He was a folk singer at the time but when his first recording was turned down by EMI he reverted (almost!) to being Mark Feld. In 1965

Decca released *The Wizard* and he became Marc Bolan. His next musical venture was a spell with 'John's Children' whom he joined in 1966. After several singles (*Desdemona* was the most well known) he left the band. Marc then palled up with percussionist Steve Peregrine Took and three other musicians. This new band was called 'Tyrannosaurus Rex.' After some musical equipment was repossessed Bolan and Took carried on as an acoustic duo. In 1967, Tony Visconti discovered them and they signed up and started to record under Visconti's tutelage. The single *Debora,* and an album *My People Were Fair And Had Sky In Their Hair But Now They're Content To Wear Stars On Their Brows* were issued and well received critically. In 1968 they laid down *Prophets, Seers, And Sages, The Angels Of The Ages.* The band's third album *Unicorn* had a more commercial feel and accessible songs. Before the fourth album Mickey Finn replaced Steve Took. In March 1970 *A Beard Of Stars* was released and almost entered the Top Ten. Later that year Marc switched to electric guitar and changed the name of the band to 'T Rex.' Bingo! A hit materialised with *Ride A White Swan.* An album entitled *T Rex* was released December 1970. Bassist Steve Currie and Bill (Fifield) Legend with the new meatier 'T Rex' topped the chart for six weeks in early 1971 with *Hot Love. Get It On* was another number one topper and their biggest hit ever. Bill also played on the album *Electric Warrior* released September of the same year. In 1972, 'T.Rex' were massive stars. Marc even had his own record label, the 'T Rex Wax Co.' In January 1972 *Telegram Sam* also hit number one. 'T.Rex' then played to sold out Wembley audiences. A compilation album *Born To Boogie* was released in April of that year. Another album *Slider* was released in July. The single *20th Century Boy* was issued 1973. In March an album called *Tanx* was released but was not as successful as other 'T Rex' LP's. At the end of 1973 Bill

Legend left 'T Rex' in the middle of an Australian tour. Bolan then began to experiment with a more soulful feel for his music with *Zinc Alloy And The Hidden Riders Of Tomorrow Or A Creamed Cage In August* which surfaced in February 1974. Marc had a burgeoning relationship with an American singer called Gloria Jones and was also becoming increasingly influenced by black music. The 'T Rex' sound was changing completely. In March of 1974 Tony Visconti and Marc parted company. Also in that year Mickey Finn left the band. By 1975 'T Rex' issued the album that was the least popular LP to date *Bolan's Zip Gun*. Marc had been living in Beverly Hills to avoid the British taxes, and had problems with drugs and alcohol. Marc cheered up when his son Rolan was born. Marc was always a fighter and returned to the UK determined to get back on top. In June 1975 a new single *New York City* was released and reached 15th in the UK chart. 'T Rex' hit the road again. In January 1976 'T.Rex' started their biggest tour of England since 1971. The album *Futuristic Dragon* was released but it only just scraped into the top 50. In June 1976 the single *I Love To Boogie* was released and this single did get to an acceptable no. 13. Steve Currie left the band at about this time. In March 1977 another LP, *Dandy In The Underworld* was issued. Things were on the up and up. But Marc died in an accident when the car driven by Gloria Jones, hit a tree on September 16th, 1977, just weeks before his 30th birthday.

22.
An Old Face And More College Gigs

In the meantime we had turned to an old face to fill the drum stool in 'Legend' and recruited Bob Clouter who fitted in very quickly as he had already played with us all in various bands before.

Legend again 1971 (L to R)
Mickey Jupp, John Bobin, Bob Clouter, Mo Witham

College gigs still proliferated like 'Queen Elizabeth College' and 'Leeds University' and we were beginning to feel very optimistic for the future of 'Legend.' By now we were all 'pro' but this did not mean that we were earning vast fortunes.

David Knights used to pay us all £10 per person, per week and keep details of how the band's finances were panning out. In point of fact we were beginning to build up a debt to David, which he obviously hoped would be repaid as our financial fortunes improved. The band was cooking however and we had finally persuaded Mickey that we should feature at least some of his songs on stage. He is (and was) a great songwriter who has now had his songs covered by all manner of singers such as Dave Edmunds, Elkie Brooks, Dr Feelgood, 'The Judds' and Gary Brooker.

23.
Moonshine and Matthew Fisher

Our next album was recorded at the 'Phillips' studio near Marble Arch. We knew that we wanted to do something different to the *Red Boot* album and Mickey obliged by furnishing very varied songs. The engineer Chris Harding helped us to produce this LP and we also had assistance from Matthew Fisher (of 'Procol Harum') who arranged the strings on three of the tracks. Matthew Fisher had already worked with Mickey Jupp on the *Georgia George* single but now turned his hand to some beautiful string arrangements for *Mother Of My Child, Another Guy* and *The Writer Of Songs.* I can still recall the thrill that we experienced when we first heard the string section playing Matthew's arrangements to our backing tracks. Although Matthew is primarily known for his main instrument, the 'Hammond' organ, he is a talented multi-instrumentalist and plays piano and other keyboards (natch!) and also guitar, bass and harmonica. He also has a good voice, which is clear and sensitive and has recorded some fine solo work in addition to his 'Procol Harum' numbers. Matthew's most famous playing has to be the signature line in *A Whiter Shade Of Pale* but he has played on six 'PH' albums and five of his own. In 1963 he was in 'Matt and the Deputies', followed by 'The Society Five'. He has also worked with David Bowie, Screaming Lord Sutch, Joe Cocker and many others.

Del Newman was the MD on *Moonshine* and he impressed

us with his super cool and laid back approach to controlling the session musicians who formed the string section. Del has worked with many top artists such as Elton John, Gordon Giltrap, Diana Ross and Leo Sayer so 'Legend' was again being looked after by a real pro.

This album was called *Moonshine* after the opening track. We asked Paul Shuttleworth who was an old friend of ours and who later had success as lead singer of 'The Kursaal Flyers' (also featuring Will Birch on drums) to design a tasteful album cover. His offering was a blue monochrome photo of moonlight shining through a forest but this great picture was turned down in favour of a horrible black and white picture of a man strolling across Westminster Bridge (I think) with a lion's head instead of his own.

'Westfield College' in Hampstead was another of the colleges that we played for. The bill here included 'The Bluenotes', 'Mandrake' and 'Mudge and Clutterbuck.' 'Mudge and Clutterbuck' was a duo from the West Country. The two members were Dave Mudge and Tim Clutterbuck (who unfortunately died in 1998.) Tim now lives in Jacksonville in Florida and he designs contact lenses for a living. I will resist the temptation to say that his favourite song is *I Can See Clearly Now*. There were some Mudge and Clutterbuck recordings including an EP and what seems to be an unreleased album made for 'Village Thing' records.

'Kings College' tried to win over the punters with a fashion show but I can't honestly say what any of the models wore.

We played 'The Marquee' again with 'UFO' and 'Brewers Droop' and their programme for that month included 'Led Zeppelin', Keef Hartley, Ashton (Gardner and Dyke), 'Mott the Hoople' and 'If.'

'UFO' was a rock band formed in 1969 by Andy Parker

(drums), Phil Mogg (vocals), Pete Way (bass) and Mick Bolton (guitar) and they were initially called 'Hocus Pocus'. They had a style that has been described as 'fused progressive space-rock and good-time boogie' (whatever that is!) Three albums came out on 'Nova-Beacon' and were successful in Germany and Japan. In 1974 Bolton was replaced by Larry Wallis, followed by Bernie Marsden and finally Michael Schenker. They moved labels to 'Chrysalis' and issued *Phenomenon*. Some other good albums followed, and the band became a five-piece in 1976, when Danny Peyronel joined on keyboards. There were other personnel changes and additional well-received albums. Schenker left in 1978 and Paul Chapman replaced him. More albums followed but these were insipid compared to the Schenker led albums. More changes occurred and a farewell UK tour was undertaken in 1983. In 1985 Mogg reformed the band with Raymond and Gray, plus bass player Paul Gray, drummer Jim Simpson, and a Japanese guitarist Atomik Tommy M. An album called *Misdemeanor* was issued but was unsuccessful. Mogg and Way went back together with guitarist Laurence Archer and drummer Clive Edwards, to record *High Stakes & Desperate Men*. This album was released in 1992 with limited success, but the fans really wanted a full reunion with Schenker. Finally this happened in 1995 with a line-up of Mogg, Schenker, Way, Raymond and Parker who recorded *Walk On Water* released at first in Japan only. This line-up, except for Parker, toured in Europe and Japan, but not always with Schenker. Drummer Aynsley Dunbar then joined Mogg, Way and Schenker.

'Brewer's Droop' was a pub-rock band from High Wycombe. Their line up initially was: Ron Watts (vocals), Steve Darrington (keyboards), John McKay (guitar), Malcolm Barret (bass) and Bob Walker (drums.) They specialised in blues/cajun and smut and were banned from many venues. Their first album issued in 1972 was called *Opening Time* ('Big Bear Records.') The second album was produced by Dave Edmunds but was not released until 1989. This LP named *The Booze Brothers,* featured Mark Knopfler and Pick Withers from 'Dire Straits.'

'If' had a superb guitarist called Geoff Whitehorn (in their second line up) who would later go on to play with 'Procol Harum', led by one my of earliest influences, the wonderful Gary Brooker.

'Mott the Hoople' later reformed with a new singer, Nigel Benjamin from Southend. Nigel had been in an earlier band with bassist Phil Mitchell who joined 'Legend' after I left and who later became the bass player for 'Dr Feelgood.' The first line up of 'Dr Feelgood' featured a young Wilko Johnson (real name John Wilkinson) and he and his fellow band members used to come to see 'Legend' when we first started. When Wilko Johnson was with 'Dr. Feelgood,' he once said of Mickey Jupp: "He's the best white singer I've ever heard and he's a great songwriter." After I left 'Legend', Wilko asked me to join a new band that he was forming and we did run through some numbers with B J (Barrie) Wilson on drums and John Potter on piano. Although I was flattered to be asked to join Wilko's new band I needed some time to get my head straight and decided form a semi pro covers band instead.

One of 'Legend's' roadies was a very nice guy called Roger Balcombe who combined these duties with running a club night in Basildon, which he called 'Asylem' (his spelling not mine) and he advertised a 'Legend' gig as 'a boozers' benefit!'

At one gig the organisers told us that they had provided us with some beer in the dressing room. We thought that this was very sporting of them until we saw that it was all brown ale. Now this was no ordinary brown ale but we had never before experienced the delights of Newcastle Brown.

This is pretty well known now but was not so widely popular in those days. We thought we would give it a try and were pleasantly surprised by its bitter yet sweet taste. We waded through several crates of this beer before we played and were brilliant. We played like we had never played before and when David came back stage to talk to us after the gig we though that he would have been very pleased with our performance. He promptly shattered that myth by telling us that we had played as if we were wearing lead gloves. The moral of the story is: 'Never underestimate the power of Newcastle Brown.'

24.
The Italian Job

*L*ife was by now a hit in Italy. It entered the top 50 at 28 and then went to no. 12 (as shown in the Italian Music Magazine – 'El Disco') and hung around for 6/7 weeks before disappearing from the Italian charts. On the strength of this success David Knights arranged a five-week tour for us, which would take in Milan and the Adriatic coast. We were told that some expenses would be paid upfront but by the time that we due to go no cash had been transferred. This should have sounded warning bells but being young, naïve and dead keen to go to Italy off we went.

Roger Balcombe and another roadie, Stuart Brooks who was also a bass player went with us. (Stuart later joined 'The Pretty Things') We drove to Italy through Europe and over the Alps, trying to keep Stuart awake and hoping that he would stop looking down at the sheer drop and would concentrate on driving. On arrival at Milan we slept over night in the railway station before pushing on to Cervia on the Adriatic coast.

We had been booked in to a small hotel and the two daughters of the hotelier; Valeria and Patricia made us very welcome. I fell for the older sister, Valeria, who was a real Italian sweetie but needless to say nothing came of it. The first club that we were due to play in was 'The Papagayo.' This was partially open air and we looked forward to moving on to other venues. Something went badly wrong. There was no money, no other gigs except a quick session in a club in Rimini and no real explanation about why we were stranded in Italy with no money and no work. When we played at 'The Yeh Yeh Club' in Rimini there were pools of water on the floor and I noticed that the resident bass player had rubber gloves on. He said that this was safety precaution; so that was obviously a nice place to play. We made the most of our time there in Cervia, about ten days or so, by swimming and trying to convince Stuart that he had swum a long way under water by moving quickly away from him once his head was submerged. Our fear was that if we went to the police or the British Consulate to explain our monetary difficulties that we might be forced to sell our gear to raise money to get home. Rather reluctantly we decided to do a moonlight flit from the friendly hotel without paying our bill. We went straight to Milan to the offices of 'Phonogram' who were the parent company of 'Phillips/Vertigo' and introduced ourselves to a bemused executive. Yes, he knew who we were. Yes, he could get us some work but no, it would not come through for several weeks. We borrowed money as advance royalties to get home from 'Phonogram' and returned to Southend with our tails between our legs. When we returned we carried on gigging at places like 'Heads' in SW7.

A specimen gig sheet from around this time looked like this:

- 22 05 'Leeds University'
- 23/27 05 Recording
- 28 05 'Mistrale Club' Beckenham
- 29 05 'Saxon Motel' Harlow
- 31 05 'Asylem' Basildon
- 1/17 06 Recording
- 18 06 'Assembly Rooms' Devon
- 19 06 'Pheasantry'

- 22 06 'New College' Oxford
- 24 06 'Leek Blues Club'
- 25 06 'Leeds University'
- 29 06 '1832 Club' Windsor
- 01 07 'Granary' Bristol
- 02 07 'Pheasantry'
- 05 07 'Letchworth Youth Centre'
- 06 07 'Fickle Pickle' Southend
- 12 07 'Aberystwyth College'
- 13 07 Italy.....................

The gig in Aberystwyth was immediately before a very long drive to southern Italy and by mutual consent we decided not to turn up for it. We phoned and said that the van had broken down and didn't feel all that guilty as we assumed that there were other groups appearing. Later on we did find out that we were the only act so our name was mud.

'The Saxon Motel' gig was a football dinner and dance for two clubs (for which we were a very strange choice.) I seem to recall that Bill Fifield had some sort of connection with one of the teams. The top attraction was Freddie Starr, who is definitely bonkers. Our main roadie for a long time was Pete Walmesley who tried to heckle Freddie Starr and came off worst! Pete had long curly hair and was very fond of the band 'Free.' He was also a champion nose picker and would lovingly smear his prize "snags" on the windscreen so he could admire them whilst he was driving. At one place where we were playing he ended up on top of the van whilst it was driven round and round in circles in the car park. I don't know why and I do now realise how dangerous this was but when you are young and daft you do these things. (By the way I am now old and daft.)

The college gigs continued and at 'New College' Oxford we again played with 'The Wild Angels' and Alan Bown – and we got our ball back! This gig also featured 'Roger Spear's Kinetic Wardrobe', 'Dudley Moore's Trio', 'The Bonzo Dog Doodah Band', a drag artist and another steel band.

'The Bonzo Dog Doodah Band' was part jazz, part psychedelic oddity. They appeared on the TV show, 'Do Not Adjust Your Set' and were formed by Rodney Slater and Roger Ruskin Spear. They were all arty types and their two main songwriters were Neil Innes (piano/guitar) and Vivian Stanshall (RIP), (trumpet and vocals.) Other reprobates from art school included 'Legs' Larry Smith, (drummer, dancer and chanteuse) and others listed in their famous offering 'The Intro and the Outro.' Their first album was *Gorilla* and this included the matchless 'Intro and the Outro' which purported to interduce each band member. This was fairly serious at the begininng but soon started to describe fantasy members including a 'very relaxed Adolf Hitler on vibes.' 'The Bonzos' had a hit in 1967 with *I'm the Urban Spaceman.* Surprisingly this was actually prodced Paul McCartney under the name of Apollo C. Vermouth. (Must have been before he started to take himself too seriously!) They were also in 'The Beatles' film 'Magical Mystery Tour.' Their songs had great titles like *Can Blue Men Sing The Whites?* The band toured in the USA with 'The Who' and performed at the Fillmore East with 'The Kinks.' Viv Stanshall (RIP) also used to do a mock striptease and Ruskin Spear had help from robots, including one that sang. It is said that their tune *The Canyons Of Your Mind* features the worst guitar solo ever recorded! Neil Innes later created 'The Beatles' parody band 'The Rutles' with Eric Idle. Stanshall appeared on Mike Oldfield's *Tubular Bells.* 'Legs' Larry Smith toured with Eric Clapton and Elton John and can be heard tap dancing on Elton's song 'Teenage Suicide'. They recorded some nine albums and were truly inspired!

Roger Ruskin-Spear was an original 'Bonzo Dog Doodah Band' member from 1966 to 1972. He also appeared on a reunion single in 1987. Roger plays virtually everything including the fool! He includes the flowing talents in his quiver of efforts:

- Tenor Saxophone,
- Trumpet,
- Xylophone,
- Bells,
- Tree Felling,
- Overstuffed Closet,
- Robots,
- The Theremin Leg,
- Clarinet,
- Guitar,
- Flageolet,
- Hookah,
- Cornet,
- Humanoid,
- Physical Extremities,
- Trouser Press, Oboe,
- Tam Tam,
- Accordion,
- Glockenspiel,
- Vocals

As well as being a Bonzo he was a member of Viv Stanshall's 'Big Grunt' and formed 'Roger Ruskin Spear & His Giant Kinetic Wardrobe'. Two albums were released *Electric Shocks* & *Unusual*. Later Roger was in 'Tatty Ollity' with Sam Spoons and a single was issued, *Punktuation/Let's Talk Basic.*) His next band was the 'The Slightly Dangerous Brothers.' He has made various guest appearances but seems to have given up music.

Dudley Moore was best known as a comedian and actor but was a truly talented pianist. He died at 66 in the United States after a long illness in 2002. He had been suffering from progressive supranuclear palsy, which attacks brain cells and impairs mental and motor functions. When he announced his illness in 1999, he joked "I understand that one person in 100,000 suffers from the disease and I am also aware that there are 100,000 members of my union, the Screen Actors Guild, who are working every day. I think, therefore, it is in some way considerate of me that I have taken on the disease for myself, thus protecting the remaining 99,999 members from this fate." He will always be remembered for the work that he did with Peter Cook and for his superb turn as the alcoholic 'Arthur.' 'Not Only -- But Also' and 'Derek and Clive' were an unlikely start for a film star but many of us will remember the 'Derek and Clive – Live' sketch that talked about 'The worst job that I ever had...' Dudley Moore won many awards during his career including Tony awards, a Grammy, two Golden Globes and an Oscar nomination. He was a musical prodigy when young and won a music scholarship to 'Magdalen College', Oxford, to study the organ. He left university an accomplished jazz pianist and performed widely before finding fame with 'Beyond The Fringe,' a comedy revue with Peter Cook, Jonathan Miller and Alan Bennett. Dudley Moore was superb that night; a really good jazz pianist and Mo had the added privilege of sitting next to his gorgeous wife Suzy Kendall. The other attractions included a circus, dodgems, a fairground a palmist and more.

'Vertigo' wanted to put out a sampler so they asked us to record a Mickey Jupp number called *Foxfield Junction*. This was an acoustic number just featuring Mickey and Mo and it was released on a compilation called *Heads Together – First Round*.

Other acts on the album, which was released in 1971 were:

- 'Jade Warrior'
- 'Sunbird'
- Jimmy Campbell
- 'Magna Carta'
- Martin Carthy
- 'Nirvana'
- 'John Dummer's Famous Music Band'
- 'Assagai' (sic)
- 'Daddy Longlegs'
- 'Clear Blue Sky'
- 'Tudor Lodge'
- Pete Atkin
- 'Lassoo'

We played at 'The Diamond Horseshoe Bar' at the end of 'Southend Pier' in September 1971 and were very well received by the audience on our home turf. 'The Diamond Horseshoe Bar' later burnt down and has never been rebuilt due to the fact that the premises were underinsured.

Another famous place at which we played was 'The Greyhound' in Fulham (where Bob Marley played in 1973.) We were also still gigging at the colleges like the' Umist' ('University of Manchester Institute of Science and Technology') Xmas Ball in 'The Barnes Wallis' building. The line up there was as follows:

- Steel band
- 'Legend'
- 'Kindness'
- 'Astora Dance Band'
- 'Spring'
- 'Graphite'
- 'Greasy Bear'

The last college gig that I did with 'Legend' was 'The Wantage Halls of Residence' but I have no record of the gig apart from knowing where it was.

I was really down after the failure of our Italian jaunt and worried about the debts that we were building up. I believe now that we should have just had a break and then started again after a short rejuvenation period but my head was not straight at the time.

I remember bursting into tears at a rehearsal to the surprise of the other guys and feeling that everybody hated me! So I decided to leave and Bob followed suit. Phil Mitchell was the new bass player and another excellent drummer Barney James replaced Bob Clouter. Barney later played with another 'Vertigo' act, 'Warhorse' and 'Rick Wakeman.' James appeared on several albums with Wakeman including *Journey to the Centre of the Earth* and *The Myths and Legends of King Arthur & The Knights of the Round Table*. Phil Mitchell later became a regular member of 'Dr. Feelgood' and has also worked with 'Love Affair.'

This was the end of an era but I have played regularly ever since in gigging bands with an occasional reunion sortie with ex 'Legend' pals. We never made the big time but I have been privileged to play with some really excellent musicians and this is my testament to their influence and friendship.

The End (Or is it?)

25.
Epilogue

This book covers a relatively short period from 1960 to 1972 but I am still playing even though I am older and greyer.

The members of 'The Phantoms' are all still around:

- "Lefty" Leftwich plays in a sixties band called 'The Flashbacks' and is also in a duo that started life as a Shadows tribute band called 'Shazam.' They have now extended their repertoire to include other suitable (old!) material. Lefty also makes fine classical guitars but be warned, they are very expensive!

- Bob Clouter has played in many bands over the years and was in a southern country rock outfit called 'Against the Grain.' Unfortunately they have now split up but they were a very good band indeed. Bob is now with another excellent band called 'The Return of the Ugly Guys' also featuring ex-'Kursaals', Paul Shuttleworth and Vic Collins.

- Mark Mills is now in Spain and I think he was beginning to get itchy fingers again the last time I heard from him.

'The Fingers' have dispersed (although we did a few reunion gigs along the way):

- Ricky Mills lives oop North and plays in a duo when he is not working as an electrician.

- Dave Grout still lives in Southend but he has sold all his gear.
- Alan Beecham is a complete musical tart! (Only joking Al!) He will play anywhere with anybody and will tackle any kind of music. Until 'The Bandstand' on Southend Cliffs was demolished he even used to do tea dances.
- Mo Witham lives in Cumbria, runs the local village band and has a recording studio. Over the years he has played with Frankie Ford, Chris Farlowe, Suzi Quatro and Sniff Pilchard.
- Bob Clouter (see above)

'Legend' have also gone their separate ways:

- Mickey Jupp has recorded some terrific albums and many other artists such as Dave Edmunds, Elkie Brooks, Delbert McClinton, 'The Judds', and Nick Lowe have used his songwriting talent.
- Mo Witham (see above)
- Bill Fifield has also worked continuously and until recently was in another band called 'Legend' with Len Tuckey (Suzi Quatro's ex-guitarist and ex-husband.)
- Bob Clouter (see above)

I have been in many bands since 1972 including 'Amber', 'Kingfisher' and 'Oscar'. I am currently in a five piece called 'In 2 Deep', the line up of which includes a wonderful keyboard player called Trevor Morgan who I have played with since 1978. 'In 2 Deep' also has a great guitarist named Denis Masterton. The other members are Steve Rayner (nice drummer!) and Eric (Billy B) Boulter who can sing anything ever written.

Occasional Rock and Roll work surfaces and Denis and I always jump at the chance to reacquaint ourselves with this, our favourite music. When we do these gigs we often play with

Mickey Brownlee who was in point of fact 'The Paramounts' original drummer.

Our Rock and Roll efforts are usually with a band called 'Hunt, Runt, Shunt and Cunningham' and this outfit is lead by the irrepressible Tony Sumner whom Gary Brooker says taught him *The Ubangi Stomp.*

Tony is another music business veteran. He was once called 'Conroy Cannon' and recorded a cover version of *Oh Happy Day* where Sue and Sunny supplied the backing vocals. So there you - are yet another coincidence in the music biz!

I am going to sign off now and as Tommy Bruce used to say:

"Now That's Rock and Roll!"

26.
Reference Sources

Notes:

- All these links worked when I researched the particular piece of information that is described in the web pages in question.
- The Internet is a movable feast. Some of these pages may have been changed, moved or no longer exist. (This is like a book going out of print!)
- If you cannot reach the information that you seek try one of the free search engines. (Use the 'advanced search' facilities.)
- Because of the age of the author some of the memories may not be crystal clear.
- Please accept these detailed reference sources as just a starter for your main course...

100 Club
http://www.the100club.co.uk/

Abbey Road
http://www.abbeyroadcafe.com/content/history.html
http://www.fabfour.addr.com/abbeyroad.htm
http://www.abbeyroad.co.uk/

Advision

http://www.sound.co.uk/www/history.htm

Alan Bown
http://www.borderlinebooks.com/uk6070s/tapestry.
html?http://www.borderlinebooks.com/uk6070s/b15.
html
http://www.vh1.com/artists/az/bown_alan/bio.jhtml

Alan Elsdon
http://www.geocities.com/sean_mccool/whoswho.html

Alan Parker
http://www.vinylvulture.co.uk/pages/t_4_tv_comps.htm

Antoinette
http://www.allmusic.com/cg/amg.dll?p=amg&uid=UID
MISS70312050531331830&sql=B11tqoauaiijp

Audience
http://www.borderlinebooks.com/uk6070s/tapestry.
html?http://www.borderlinebooks.com/uk6070s/a7.html

Barry Fantoni
http://www.cyber-nation.com/victory/quotations/authors/
quotes_fantoni_barry.html
http://www.bbc.co.uk/comedy/guide/articles/g/
grubstreet_1299001333.shtml

Bert Weedon
http://www.bertweedon.com/biog.htm

Big Jim Sullivan

http://bigjimsullivan.com/

Billy Fury
http://www.billyfury.com/

Binson Echorec
http://www.binson.com/

Bob and Marcia
http://www.xs4all.nl/~bobandy/bobbio.htm
http://www.vh1.com/artists/az/griffiths_marcia/bio.jhtml

Bob Marley
http://www.bobmarleymagazine.com/didyouknow/did1.
htm

Bonzo Dog Doo-Dah Band
http://en.wikipedia.org/wiki/Bonzo_Dog_Doo-Dah_
Band

Breakaways The
http://www.vickibrown.co.uk/Breakaways.html

Brewer's Droop
http://www.neck-and-neck.com/library/biographies/
brewers.html

Carol Elvin
http://www.artistdirect.com/store/artist/
album/0,,1139901,00.html

Changing Strings

http://www.visionmusic.com/questionmark.html
http://www.musicianforums.com/forums/showthread/t-120467.html

Circus Days
http://www.marmalade-skies.co.uk/strange.htm

Clem Cattini
http://members.lycos.co.uk/cattinidrummer/

Cliff Bennett
http://www.theiceberg.com/artist/24916/cliff_bennett.html

Climax Chicago Blues Band The
http://members.tripod.com/rant58/id354.htm

CND
http://www.cnduk.org/index.html

Creation The
http://www.makingtime.co.uk/creation.html

Daddy Longlegs
http://www.borderlinebooks.com/uk6070s/tapestry.html?http://www.borderlinebooks.com/uk6070s/d1.html

Dallas Tuxedo
http://www.primrosehillrecords.com/books/reviews/17w-bassist07-97.html
http://liverpoolbeatlescene.com/Tuxedo.html

Dave Dee, Dozy, Beaky, Mick and Titch
http://freespace.virgin.net/dd.dbmt/dozybiog.htm

Dave Mattacks
http://www.dmattacks.co.uk/

Dave Travis
http://members.tripod.com/hoppula/europeanrock.htm
http://www.xs4all.nl/~boekglas/MartinKaye/K234.JPG

David Essex
http://www.davidessex.com/biography/

David Garrick
http://www.amazon.co.uk/exec/obidos/search-handle-form/202-6875060-4949401
http://www.borderlinebooks.com/uk6070s/tapestry.html?http://www.borderlinebooks.com/uk6070s/g1z.html

Del Newman
http://www.artistdirect.com/music/artist/card/0,,473110,00.html

Denmark Street
http://www.coventgarden.uk.com/denmark.html

Don Storer and Cherry Wainer
http://www.fortunecity.com/greenfield/wolf/31/id60.htm
http://www.fortunecity.com/greenfield/wolf/31/id57.htm

Dr. Feelgood
http://www.theiceberg.com/artist/31539/dr_feelgood.html

Early Days of Rock The
http://www.blazemonger.com/GG/albums/dupree/early.
days.of.rock.v1.html

Eel Pie Island
http://www.eelpieclub.com/

Emperor Rosko
http://www.emperorrosko.com/

Episode Six
http://www.artistdirect.com/music/artist/
card/0,,427877,00.html

Equals The
http://www.artistdirect.com/music/artist/
bio/0,,427924,00.html?artist=The+Equals

Flies The
http://www.borderlinebooks.com/uk6070s/tapestry.
html?http://www.borderlinebooks.com/uk6070s/f6z.html

Force Five
http://www.borderlinebooks.com/uk6070s/tapestry.
html?http://www.borderlinebooks.com/uk6070s/f7z.html

Futurama
http://www.steverussell.freeserve.co.uk/hofner/futurama/
fut.html

Geoff Stephens

http://www.peermusic.com/artistpage/Geoff_Stephens.
html

Geoff Whitehorn
http://www.borderlinebooks.com/uk6070s/tapestry.html

Georgia George
http://www.procolharum.com/jupp_fs.htm

Gods The
http://www.collecting-tull.com/TullTree/Gods.html
http://www.micktaylor.net/

Hedgehoppers Anonymous
http://www.45-rpm.org.uk/dirh/hedgehoppersa.htm
http://www.borderlinebooks.com/uk6070s/tapestry.
html?http://www.borderlinebooks.com/uk6070s/h5z.html

Heinz Burt
http://www.guardian.co.uk/obituaries/
story/0,3604,178811,00.html

Hohner Pianet
http://www.harmony-central.com/Synth/Data/Hohner/
Pianet-L-01.html

Hopf Guitars
http://store.bluebookinc.com/downloads/BrowseCategory.
asp?Product=electricguitar&Heading=449

Human Instinct The

http://www.artistdirect.com/music/artist/
bio/0,,857520,00.html?artist=The+Human+Instinct

Hunters The
http://www.45-rpm.org.uk/artists-h.htm

Ian Gibbons
http://www.geocities.com/SunsetStrip/Diner/2674/igibb_
b.htm

Irish Slang
http//www.redbrick.dcu.ie/~icecream/stuff/faq/
tedfaq0.54.html#1.06

Jackie Edwards
http://www.musicweb.uk.net/encyclopaedia/e/E17.HTM

James Burton
http://www.telecaster.demon.co.uk/docs/jb.htm

Jess Conrad
http://www.onestopents.com/jess.htm

Joe Brown
http://www.joebrown.co.uk/frames_ie.asp

John Carter
http://www.peermusic.com/artistpage/John_Carter.html

John Pantry
http://www.borderlinebooks.com/uk6070s/tapestry.

html?http://www.borderlinebooks.com/uk6070s/comps/
c_21_001.html

Jonathan King
http://www.kingofhits.com/

Julie Felix
http://www.knibb.org/juliefelix/biography.htm

Keef Hartley Big Band The
http://www.borderlinebooks.com/uk6070s/tapestry.
html?http://www.borderlinebooks.com/uk6070s/h3z.
html

Kinks The
http://www.borderlinebooks.com/uk6070s/tapestry.
html?http://www.borderlinebooks.com/uk6070s/k4.html

Koobas The
http://www.geocities.com/fabgear6366/koobas.htm
http://www.borderlinebooks.com/uk6070s/tapestry.
html?http://www.borderlinebooks.com/uk6070s/k5z.
html

Kursaal Fyers The
http://www.theiceberg.com/artist/27409/kursaal_flyers.
html
http://www.kursaalflyers.net/home.php

Leslie Speakers
http://theatreorgans.com/hammond/faq/hammond-faq.
html#SEC23

Little Free Rock
http://www.illingworth70.freeserve.co.uk/

Long John Baldry
http://www.johnbaldry.com/
http://www.4starbiz.com/missdeal/baldry.htm

Manfred Mann
http://www.srv.net/~roxtar/manfred_mann.html
http://www.geocities.com/MotorCity/Garage/1291/
manfredmann.html
http://www.borderlinebooks.com/uk6070s/tapestry.
html?http://www.borderlinebooks.com/uk6070s/m2z.
html

Marmalade
http://www.borderlinebooks.com/uk6070s/tapestry.
html?http://www.borderlinebooks.com/uk6070s/m4.html

Marty Wilde
http://www.martywilde.com/index1.html
http://www.surefire.uk.com/marty.htm

Matthew Fisher
http://www.procolharum.com/procolmf.htm

Maximum Sound
http://www.unityaudio.co.uk/thermionic_culture_site/
mr_thermionic.htm

Maze The

http://www.thehighwaystar.com/rosas/jouni/re.html

Merseybeats The and Merseys The
http://www.45-rpm.org.uk/dirm/merseybeats.htm

Mick Green
http://www.artistdirect.com/music/artist/
card/0,,438175,00.html

Mickie Most
http://entertainment.msn.com/artist/?artist=711345

Mods
http://groups.msn.com/TheSixtiesPleasureZone/
yourwebpage6.msnw

Monty Python's Flying Circus
http://www.museum.tv/archives/etv/M/htmlM/
montypython/montypython.htm

Mooche
http://www.borderlinebooks.com/uk6070s/tapestry.
html?http://www.borderlinebooks.com/uk6070s/p6.html

Moog Synthesisers
http://www.obsolete.com/120_years/machines/moog/

Monotones The
http://www.borderlinebooks.com/uk6070s/tapestry.
html?http://www.borderlinebooks.com/uk6070s/m11.
html

Move The
http://www.themoveonline.com/history.html

Mudge and Clutterbuck
http://www.martin-kingsbury.co.uk/articles/
mudge&clutterbuck.htm
http://www.martin-kingsbury.co.uk/articles/
village%20thing.htm

My Kinda Life
http://members.tripod.com/~weejock/index-6.html
http://www.runemoe.com/bruceproducer.xls

Nashville Teens
http://www.nashville-teens.com/indfa.htm

Neil Christian
http://www.theiceberg.com/artist/27933/neil_christian.
html

Nicky Hopkins
http://store.artistdirect.com/music/artist/
bio/0,,445470,00.html?artist=Nicky+Hopkins

Paramounts The
http://www.procolharum.com/99/p/jomo_EP_
paramounts_uk.jpg

Patrick Kerr
http://www.procolharum.com/yan_para%5E2.htm

Peter and the Wolves

http://www.borderlinebooks.com/uk6070s/tapestry.
html?http://www.borderlinebooks.com/uk6070s/p4.html

Peter Eden
http://www.girecords.com/lpep.htm

Pheasantry The
http://www.uktravelbureau.com/regions/england/
chelsea2.cfm
http://theband.hiof.no/albums/food_of_love.html
http://www.smh.com.au/articles/2003/08/29/1062050659
087.html
http://www.jpost.com/Editions/2001/03/28/Food/
Recipes.23756.html

Pinkerton's (Assorted) Colours
http://www.geocities.com/fabgear6366/pinkerton.htm

Psychedelia at Abbey Road
http://images.google.co.uk/imgres?imgurl=www.
artistdirect.com/Images/Sources/AMGCOVERS/
music/cover200/drd700/d731/d73163sik29.
jpg&imgrefurl=http://www.artistdirect.com/store/artist/
album/0,,372725,00.html&h=200&w=200&prev=/imag
es%3Fq%3Dpsychedelia%2Bat%2Babbey%2Broad%26s
vnum%3D10%26hl%3Den%26lr%3D%26ie%3DUTF-
8%26oe%3DUTF-8%26as_qdr%3Dall

Purple Hearts
http://www.milesago.com/Artists/Purplehearts.htm

Ray McVay

http://www.glennmillerorchestra.co.uk/ray.htm

Red Boot Album
http://images.google.co.uk/imgres?imgurl=home.online.
no/~frodebye/mickey_jupp/thumbnails/cd_red_boot.
jpg&imgrefurl=http://home.online.no/~frodebye/
mickey_releases.htm&h=100&w=100&prev=/images%
3Fq%3Dred%2Bboot%2B%2522legend%2522%26sv
num%3D10%26hl%3Den%26lr%3D%26ie%3DUTF-
8%26oe%3DUTF-8%26sa%3DN%26as_qdr%3Dall
http://images.google.co.uk/imgres?imgurl=www.
collectable-records.ru/images/GROUPS/legend/
red%2520boot/front.jpg&imgrefurl=http://
www.collectable-records.ru/groups/legend/
&h=219&w=231&prev=/images%3Fq%3D%2B%2522l
egend%2Bred%2Bboot%2522%26svnum%3D10%26h
l%3Den%26lr%3D%26ie%3DUTF-8%26oe%3DUTF-
8%26sa%3DN%26as_qdr%3Dall

Renaissance
http://www.borderlinebooks.com/uk6070s/tapestry.
html?http://www.borderlinebooks.com/uk6070s/r3.html

Revolution Club The
http://twtd.bluemountains.net.au/cream/freshlive.htm

Rhet Stoller
Sleeve notes from "Ember Lane" CD issued 1992 (See For
Miles Records Ltd.) (Originally issued by Chapter One
Records Ltd. 1972.)

Rick Wakeman

http://www.artistdirect.com/store/artist/album/
full/0,,506656,00.html

Roger Ruskin Spear
http://www.neilinnes.org/scroger.htm

Ronnie Scott's
http://www.ronniescotts.co.uk/ronnie_scotts/ronniescotts/
pics/history.htm

Root and Jenny Jackson
http://www.soulbrother.co.uk/fbi.htm

Roy Young
http://www.royyoung.com/

Scotch of St. James The
http://www.angelfire.com/music3/sentstarr/scotch.html
http://www.music.indiana.edu/som/courses/rock/misc.
html
http://jimihendrix13.tripod.com/mainfolder/1966.htm
http://www.theguitarists.galaxyhit.com/Jimioct.html

Screaming Lord Sutch
http://www.borderlinebooks.com/uk6070s/tapestry.
html?http://www.borderlinebooks.com/uk6070s/s18.html

Selmer
http://www.donmack.com/SelmerLondon.htm

Shadows The

http://www.malcolmcampbell.me.uk/reviews/review1.
html
http://www.mcr26.freeserve.co.uk/
"Twang" sleeve notes. CD issued 1996 by PANG/EA
Records UK

Skindles Hotel
http://www.maidenhead.net/history/

Shakin Stevens
http://www.shakinstevens.com/

Simon Dupree
http://www.theiceberg.com/artist/26429/simon_dupree.
html

Slade
http://members.aol.com/brianr7651/Slade/His1.html

Sounds Around
http://www.borderlinebooks.com/uk6070s/tapestry.
html?http://www.borderlinebooks.com/uk6070s/s10.html

Sounds Incorporated
http://www.fretmusic.co.uk/liveguide/articles/Sounds.
htm

Sue and Sunny
http://www.loadofold.com/boots/sunny_disc.html

Symbols
http://www.borderlinebooks.com/uk6070s/tapestry.

html?http://www.borderlinebooks.com/uk6070s/s19z.
html

Tapestry of Delights
http://www.borderlinebooks.com/uk6070s/tapestry.html
Time and time again the website that has come up trumps
has been "The Tapestry of Delights." If you want to know
about U.K. psych, beat and progressive music between
1963 - 1976. This e-book contains band histories/musical
analysis on over 3,400 UK acts of the era with personnel and
discographical information, where known. Also included
are listings of over 375 compilations, and over 1,100 sleeve
illustrations. This site is absolutely phenomenal and if you
prefer it, you can order the mammoth hard copy book by
Vernon Joynson.

Taste
http://www.hotshotdigital.com/WellAlwaysRemember/
RorysBio.html

T Rex
http://home.earthlink.net/~apawlo/jblbiography.html

Ten Years After
http://alvinlee.com/biography.html
http://www.sing365.com/music/lyric.nsf/singerUnid/
1054C988CA157E834825698B000C788A

Tenth Planet
http://www.marmalade-skies.co.uk/planet.htm

Tommy Bruce

http://www.cherryred.co.uk/rpm/rpm/tommybruce.htm

Tommy Vance
http://uproar.fortunecity.com/galaxy/399/tommyv.htm

Tony Blackburn
http://www.mpce.com/blackburn.htm

Tony Visconti
http://www.tonyvisconti.com
www.procolharum.com

Tremeloes The
http://www.nostalgiacentral.com/music/tremeloes.htm

UFO
http://www.vh1.com/artists/az/ufo/bio.jhtml

Unit 4 + 2
http://www.artistdirect.com/music/artist/
bio/0,,504361,00.html?artist=Unit+4%2B2

Vernon Haddock's Jubilee Lovelies
http://www.borderlinebooks.com/uk6070s/tapestry.
html?http://www.borderlinebooks.com/uk6070s/h1.html

Vince Eager
http://www.vinceeager.co.uk/

Vox Amps
http://www.voxamps.co.uk/history/chapter_01.htm
http://www.valveamps.com/ac10twin.htm

Vox Continental Organs
http://www.alphaentek.com/vox.htm
http://users.aol.com/KeyMuseum/vox.html

Watkins Amps and Guitars
http://www.wemwatkins.co.uk/

Watkins Copicat
http://users.argonet.co.uk/users/steverussell/hofner2/copy.
html

Watkins Electric Music
http://www.wemwatkins.co.uk/story1.htm

Wild Angels The
http://www.rockabilly.nl/artists/wildangels.htm

Zombies The
http://launch.yahoo.com/artist/artistFocus.
asp?artistID=1030410
Bark Staving Ronkers

By John Bobin

2 Highfield Crescent
Rayleigh
Essex
SS6 8JP

Tel: 01268 770484

Word count: Approximately 52,000 including reference sources.